GARDEN SPACES

Simple Solutions for Planning and Design

GARDEN SPACES

Simple Solutions for Planning and Design

George Carter
Photography by Marianne Majerus

MITCHELL BEAZLEY

Garden Spaces
George Carter

First published in Great Britain in 2005 by Mitchell Beazley,
an imprint of Octopus Publishing Group Limited,
2–4 Heron Quays, London E14 4JP.

First published in paperback 2007.

© Octopus Publishing Group Limited 2005

A CIP catalogue record for this book is available
from the British Library.

ISBN-13: 978 1 84533 307 2
ISBN-10: 1 84533 307 1

While all reasonable care has been taken during the
preparation of this edition, neither the publisher,
editors, nor the authors can accept responsibility for any
consequences arising from the use thereof or from the
information contained therein.

All the illustrations in this book are by George Carter

Commissioning Editor: Michèle Byam
Executive Art Editor: Sarah Rock
Designer: Vivienne Brar
Editor: Joanna Chisholm
Photography: Marianne Majerus
Production: Gary Hayes
Index: Sue Farr

Printed and bound in China by
Toppan Printing Company Limited

Contents

Introduction

Garden Spaces sets out to illustrate and describe the many ways that a basic garden plot can be organized to produce quite different effects. It offers creative and imaginative ways to transform the look of an existing garden, or to create an entirely new one. Small gardens can be made to look larger and more spacious, and oddly shaped gardens can be turned to good advantage. Unpleasant visual pollution can be screened. In fact this book offers a series of inventive ideas for those difficult spaces with which many gardeners have to contend.

Of course, to formulate any rule is to open oneself to criticism and disagreement, but there are certain common problems in the designing of gardens that can be overcome by the application of simple guidelines. Sometimes there are several quite different ways of looking at the same problem.

The book aims to give advice at the very first level of designing a garden: formulating the basic layout – the plan, elevation, and three-dimensional arrangement of form. This is the level at which many people falter or lack confidence, yet it is crucial to both the hard-landscaping and the planting. It is the substructure of the garden on which everything else is built, diversified, or planted.

This book therefore addresses the little-considered issue that successful garden layouts rely very largely on the way the volumes and voids created by planting and hard-landscaping are organized. Because I have been trained as a sculptor, I take a particular interest in this "sculptural" approach to garden design in my own work as a garden designer.

Rather than propose rules in the abstract, *Garden Spaces* offers solutions to a series of common-place problems, in the belief that this will make the book much easier to use. Many of these solutions boil down to visual trickery and are culled from disciplines other than gardening – notably the theatre, painting, sculpture, architecture, or the study of perspective. They have always been an inspiration to gardeners, and all the theoreticians of the past from Alexander Pope to Humphry Repton to Geoffrey Jellicoe and beyond have delved into these areas for inspiration and help.

Whether you are looking for ways to link up and make sense of a series of separate garden elements which have grown up more-or-less by chance, or are trying to rethink the underlying structure of your garden, or are possibly starting to plan a garden completely from scratch, this book will give you assistance and inspiration.

◄ Foil for complex, informal planting
Even the wildest gardens need plain areas to provide contrast to busy, intricate beds. In this garden, an unadorned, white-painted wall as well as the wall of a garden building offset the bold foliage of a fig and free-form planting.

► Informal planting in a clearly defined space
This overview of a small town garden incorporates many of the ideas covered in this book: it includes contrasting light and dark foliage; a boundary that is obscured by planting; and the creation of vistas and viewstoppers. All such features are set within a partially hidden, geometric framework.

The feeling of expectation and surprise in a garden seldom happens by accident; it has to be created. Even the tiniest urban plot can be successfully subdivided. Paradoxically, the division of small spaces into even smaller ones can create the illusion of greater extent than actually exists. The real boundaries of the garden become unclear, and you catch glimpses of areas that might only be hinted at but which greatly increase the apparent space. Such a notion applies to gardens small and large, formal and informal.

Some of the design questions posed are rather nebulous and are no more defined than "where do I start?" For example, what ground or fencing material to go for is a basic question with which all gardeners have to grapple. The answer could be defined by one or more of the topics treated in this book; maybe a particular material will make the space look bigger or will reflect most light.

Under more specific headings there are solutions to the functional aspects of garden-making: how to incorporate garden buildings; and how to include all of the often-disparate uses that a garden can be put to – flower garden, vegetables, play area, storage, workshop, and outdoor living-room, for example – without the whole lacking a sense of coordination and style or containing odd juxtapositions.

Loose planting on a strongly structured framework
A screen of posts and brick-retained levels create the spatial interest in this garden. A waterwork terminating the main axis is positioned horizontally to emphasize the width of the garden. A vertical viewstopper would have given quite a different feel to the space.

The best way to use *Garden Spaces* will be to "consult the genius of the place" as the 18th-century garden pundit Alexander Pope put it. In a modern context, this could mean weighing up all the good and bad points that a garden possesses, however prosaic they might appear. They will be apparent even where there is no garden at all and you are starting with a virgin site.

Questions you might ask yourself on the plus side are "what is the best aspect?" "Where is the daylight good?" "Where are the best views out of the garden, and what are the best views from the windows of the house?" On the minus side, look at peculiar shapes of garden left by buildings and their random extensions, the nastiest views, places overlooked by neighbours, and the darkest, dankest spots. All these have a bearing on planning the layout of the garden. Don't perceive the negative points just as problems – quite often they give the garden that quirkiness which in the end proves its greatest success. Often it is these very basic factors that will give you the impetus to make decisions on a whole host of questions.

In planning a garden of any size you need to start with a "broad-brush" approach, designing the simplest, big-scale features first and only considering the small-scale detail much later. If the "bones" are right, everything else that follows is more likely to be successful. It is also the bones – the paving, the fencing, the structure planting of trees, shrubs, and hedges – that cost most money, so you need to get them right first time.

To start with, do not be afraid of bold scale and extreme simplicity. Elaboration can always come later. Even very small gardens can cope with one huge, over-scaled object or plant, particularly in the foreground of a scene. They occupy a space interestingly and grab the attention, distracting the eye from any shortcomings of size in the actual plot.

Throughout this book reference is made to the traditional painters' device of dividing up a landscape into foreground, middle ground, and distance. It is not new to apply these artificial distinctions to the design of actual gardens and their surroundings. The 18th-century landscaper Humphry Repton used the idea in both large landscape parks and in smaller gardens. It is, however, an idea that I think particularly well adapted to even very small gardens – helping the eye to recognize space and providing definition to specific areas. Several chapters deal with ways of defining these notional distinctions using both planting and hard-landscaping.

The ideas presented in this book are culled from more than 20 years of professional garden designing, and hopefully they will help remove the terrible indecision that can make starting a new garden or changing an old one such a trial.

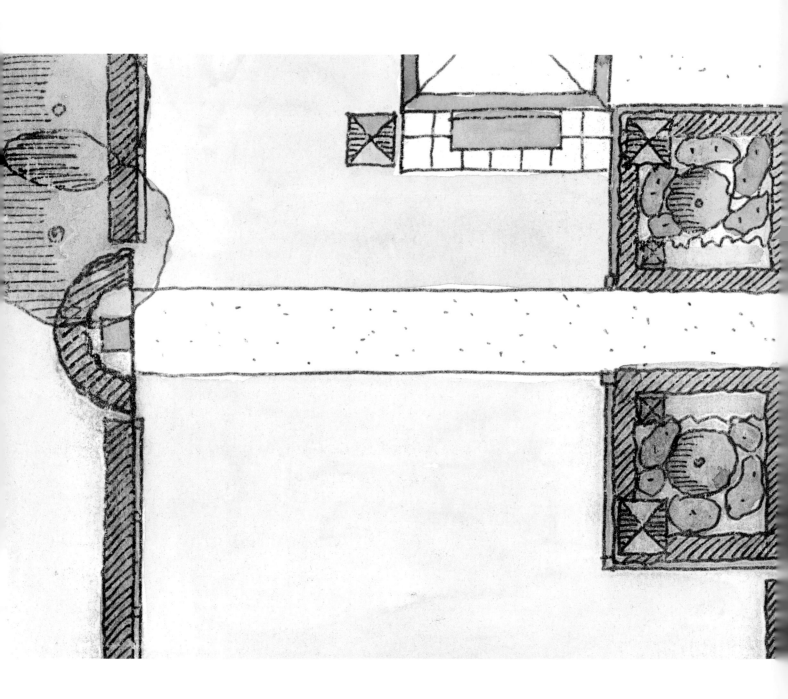

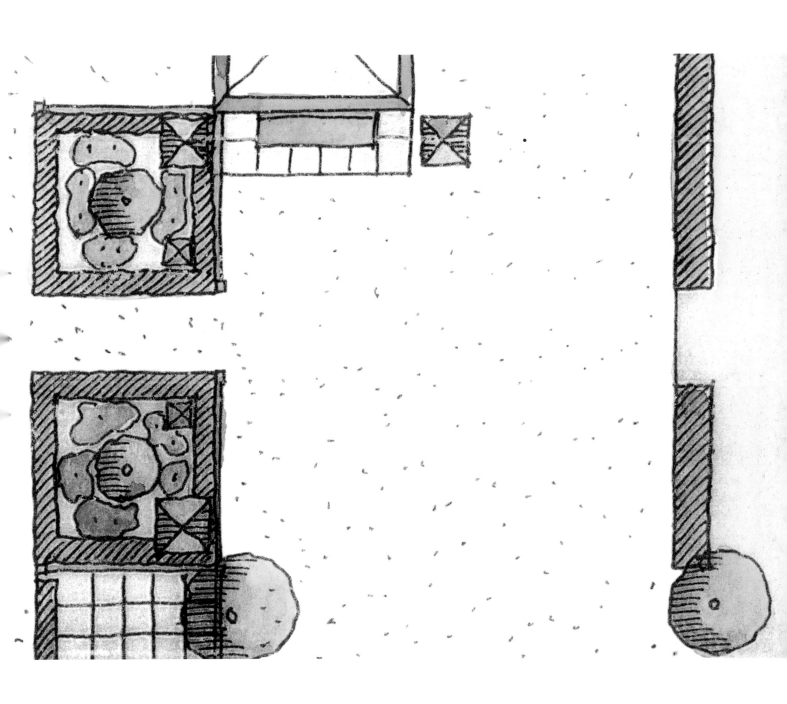

The Plan

Dividing up a plot to maximize the space

Creating an axis

Make the most of even the smallest garden site by opening up one or more vistas to the farthest limits. Create linear views to take advantage of the full width, length, or diagonal of a plot.

Creating a view or primary scene in a garden can be likened to composing a picture. As in painting, it is useful to try and provide a foreground, middle ground, and distance however confined the space. This can be achieved by devising artificial divisions – the "distance" may be only 6m (20ft) away, but if it is clearly defined it will work as the termination of your view in the way that a distant prospect works in a landscape by being framed by closer elements.

To create an axis, the eye must have an object or goal. Start by thinking where and what this should be. It might take the form of a sculpture or urn or even a small building; alternatively, it might be a distinctive plant or tree that stands well on its own. Whatever the focal point is, it must be clearly defined and have a strong, distinct outline. Remember that in nature, distant objects tend to be blue/grey – a result of particles in the atmosphere that affect the perception of colour. For this reason it is better to avoid "hot", red/orange colours in your viewstopper as they tend to jump forward visually.

The line of the axis needs to be decided in relation to the best features of the site – maybe the line should be directed towards the most open view, where the vista may act as a frame, or it could be aligned towards a view or object actually beyond your own garden. Alternatively, if you are placing a viewstopper within your own site, and if it is big enough, it could be placed so that it hides a defect – a neighbour's shed or intrusive window, for example. The goal of the view or vista may not need to be a single object – it could be a change of scene such as a shaded plantation of trees or shrubs, or a planting of different character.

The primary vista ought to start from a point in the garden which will be constantly in sight – maybe a view from the sitting-room or kitchen window or from a prime seating position on a terrace or balcony.

The visual movement towards a view can be created in a number of ways. The simplest way is perhaps to mow a straight line of shorter grass between the two points, or to follow the line of a

What is an axis?

- All gardens need primary scenes – views across them that terminate in a principal object or plant.

- This principal view can run in any direction across the width of a garden, along its length, or even diagonally. The siting is decided by the position of the best feature or features.

- The axis of a vista can be marked in many ways – simple or complex – perhaps a change in mowing line, or the route of a path, or the space between beds.

- Vistas can also be delineated by providing a view with a foreground frame which focuses the eye on an object.

- To maximize on the apparent size of a small plot, place your viewstopper on or near the edge of the site.

◄ Directing the eye
A garden can contain any number of axes, but in a small space the number should be confined. The axes should draw attention to the garden's best features or best prospects, such as an existing tree or a good view, or be something that you have created.

► Emphasis on length
This L-shaped garden has two axes at right angles to each other. The main one is defined by narrow rills of water which terminate in a baroque, fake gateway; the other axis is defined by a plain, gravel path.

▲ Economic solution
One of the simplest methods of defining an axis is to lead the eye via a change in mowing height. Here a serpentine-mown path flanked by willow or hazel hoops leads the eye across a flowery mead to a shadier part of the garden.

▼ Channelling the eye
This small town garden has a long, narrow central lawn leading to a hornbeam arbour. The flanking box-edged beds define the vista, which goes through to an urn at the back of the garden. Such a viewstopper at the farther limits of the site makes the most of a confined space.

▶ Taming a wild garden
A wide, straight mown path flanked by long grass here formalizes a wild part of a garden and creates a vista. The simple sundial provides sufficient ornament to this "undressed" setting. Its light colour contrasts well against the shady background.

path. However moving the eye in a certain direction doesn't necessarily rely on a straight line, and vistas are just as important in informal gardens: serpentine, or curved, lines can be just as effective, providing they terminate in a definite visual goal.

A vista does not necessarily rely on a visual movement at ground level such as a path or mowing line – it can be created by one or a series of frames. Think of flanking a view by a pair of dark trees, a pair of masonary or timber piers, a planted arch, or other similar device. The point is made more forcefully if there is more than one pair of framing devices – one set in the foreground, another in the middle ground, for example.

You can have fun devising vistas that cross each other and are visible only from particular parts of the garden. They would also help to create that important element of surprise which is essential to successful gardens.

If you are planning a garden from scratch, it can be difficult in a featureless plot to know where to start and where to terminate a vista, but even in the most bland piece of earth you can be inspired

by a study of the basic contours of the plot and developing your ideas from them. The principal windows that overlook the garden will give you the starting-off point for a vista. Then if nothing else exists think of the aspect of the plot. The direction it faces will have significant impact on the way light falls across the site and may give you a clue as to where to terminate a vista. A direct west-facing view would mean strong backlighting to an object in the evening, creating perhaps an interesting silhouette. Conversely, an east-facing view would be attractively front lit in the evening. However slight the hint these site-specific considerations provide, they should be useful in formulating your ideas.

◄ Simple design device
Paving slabs set in mown grass provide directional movement across a lawn. Two carved stone sculptures create a foreground entrance to the scene and mark the beginning of the vista.

▼ A change of direction
The sense of directional movement along the length of this path is enhanced by brick steps and risers which also give it pace. A pot with a strong outline provides a visual full stop and marks a change of direction in the path, suggesting further views to come.

Establishing a sense of spaciousness

There are many ways to make a space seem larger than it really is. Carry ground surfaces in a single material to the utmost limits of the site, at the same time simplify and concentrate planting schemes.

Perhaps the easiest solution in a very small garden space is to pave or deck the entire plot to the perimeter, leaving only tiny pockets of soil for plants or even restricting planting solely to containers. To maximize the visible floor area, flower beds should be concentrated in the extreme edges of the garden or confined to a single simple shape.

When deciding on ground surfaces, select materials with only a slight texture and a unified colour, because it is better to avoid a mixture of surface textures and colours in a small area. A single sweep of one material with joints that are flush and narrow will, as a rule, make for a more spacious effect. In a very small space, such as a roof terrace, cladding the parapet walls or fences and the floor in the same material and colour can help simplify and enlarge the appearance of the site.

You can counteract the effect of a long, thin site or a short, wide one by running lines at floor level along the shortest dimension. Thus decking in a short garden should run with the planks along the smaller extent to give the illusion of greater length; the narrow lines of the joints and grooves of the timber forming a direction for the eye to follow, distracting it from perceiving the excessive width and making the most of the short length. If you choose paving, run its coursed lines in the same direction to gain a similar effect. The converging perspective lines of the joints creates an illusion of greater length. The same idea can be adopted with wall surfaces: for example, a trellis with the laths running along the wall will increase its apparent length (see right).

Although design rules are made to be broken, in general boldly textured materials should be avoided: in a confined space, use the smallest grade of pea gravel – 1cm (½in) and below – rather than coarse gravel. The smooth surface of cut or cast stone will work better than a boldly riven surface. For the same reason, contrastingly veined or diversely coloured stone should be avoided in favour of even colours.

However it would be wrong to take the preference for the diminutive too rigorously. Nothing, to my mind, is more effective in a very confined space than one or a pair of boldly overscaled objects, such as urns, piers, or pieces of sculpture. These work

◄ Illusory width

A single surface extended from side to side across a narrow site will increase its apparent width. Continue this horizontal emphasis across the end boundary and emphasize it with bands of planting that break up the space.

▲ Linear effects

The use of strong parallel lines in decking and wall cladding helps expand the apparent width and depth of this tiny garden. Taking the ground treatment as far as possible to the full dimensions of the site also helps maximize the effect of spaciousness. Raised decking around two sides provides a lot of seating without cluttering up the space. Planting is strictly limited to narrow perimeter beds.

Design techniques

■ As far as possible, keep what ground space there is uninterrupted by flower beds or changes of material.

■ Where flower beds are essential, concentrate them at the edges of the garden.

■ Counteract the effect of a long, thin site or a short, wide one by aligning decking or paving along the shortest dimension of the plot.

■ Avoid fussy planting of mixed colour and texture in favour of bold masses in a single colour.

◄ Tree-lined vista
The width of the gravel forecourt in front of this modernist building is designed to relate to the width of the glass wall. Its spacious sweep is interrupted only by a single, clear-stemmed tree gravelled up to its trunk. Pleached limes on the left look good with the geometry of the architecture, and enhance the sense of movement through space.

▼ "Fitted-carpet" paving
This bird's-eye view of a small town garden shows the effect of paving right to the edges of the site with narrow beds on only two sides. Pots and containers are kept to the edges to maximize space. The plain, white walls also assist the uncluttered feeling in the garden.

▲ Formal framework
A highly controlled, geometric arrangement of
planting, paving, and low walls make the most of this
small site. Concentrated blocks of planting on only
one side of the garden act as a foil for the minimalist
nature of the architecture, and half-hidden views
suggest spaces beyond what is seen.

especially well if placed quite close to the principal viewpoint – be it
a window or terrace. They form an effective dark frame to even the
most confined prospect and throw the remaining, simplified layout,
especially if lighter in colour, into sharp perspective.

Large plants such as trees or shrubs should if possible be clear-
stemmed to the base 60–90cm (2–3ft), so the ground surface is
uninterrupted. Leave as small a visible pocket of soil around the
stem or trunk as possible, perhaps dressing the bed with a gravel or
mulch of similar colour to the main paving or other ground material.
Narrow-based, fastigiate trees and shrubs are particularly useful in
this context, adding height to the scene without taking up ground

space. Place these taller plants towards the perimeters of the site,
reserving lower-growing plants for the centre.

In general, avoid fussy planting of mixed colour and texture – a
strongly themed colour scheme such as all-grey or blue (the
recessive colours) will work better in a smaller space than
cacophonous mixtures of loud, "hot" colours. However such "hot",
orange- or red-flowered plants could be used, if desired, in the
closest foreground of the scene to intensify the recession of the
cooler colours beyond. For similar visual reasons, use boldly
textured, large-leaved foliage plants in the foreground, and
smoother-textured, smaller-leaved plants in the background.

Reflective surfaces
It is the contrast between geometry and irregularity that makes so many different kinds of garden successful. Here the sense of space is a product of the reflective qualities of light walls and paving with still water mirroring the sky. The planting – all of similar height set under clear-stemmed trees – also gives a broad, spacious sweep to the whole scene.

Establishing a sense of spaciousness 23

Dividing a plot diagonally

Although the average garden plot is rectangular in plan, there are occasions when dividing the plot diagonally makes for a more dynamic and unexpected visual effect.

With one bold stroke it is possible to transform even the blandest space. Instead of perceiving a ground plan in rectilinear terms or right angles, think in terms of 45 degrees or even more acute angles. Break up the space with a simple diagonal division and you at once make possible a whole new range of possibilities. Firstly, you probably divert the eye to a corner – which maybe the best direction rather than at a building directly in front of you; secondly you make an interesting possibility for a service area and a "front-of-house area" – every garden needs the former, however small. In addition you create dynamic movement across a space: generally diagonal compositions make for visual movement, whereas rectilinear ones create a more restful, static effect. The precise position of the diagonal determines the size of the two areas you are defining.

Having made this basic compositional decision, the next step is to decide how to project this idea upwards from plan into three dimensions. Start by creating a vertical division along or around this line: it can form a see-through screen, for example of trellis, or a solid one of hedging or boarded fencing. This vertical surface will form a new background for the more detailed planting or ornamentation of the garden. Everything will be informed by this new line – steps, paved or hard surfaces, the line of borders, planting, and so on. Obviously there need to be openings in this new division, both for

Diagonally divided garden
This garden has been given a new dynamic by being split diagonally by a 1.8m (6ft) trellis screen. The perimeter boundary on the right has been similarly treated with trellis. Such a division creates a service area to the left, which could be used for a variety of purposes such as growing vegetables, making compost, or having a children's play space. The area to the right of the division can meanwhile provide a smarter, main view from the house.

Why diagonals?

■ Subdividing even the smallest area paradoxically makes it feel larger.

■ Diagonal lines in a garden composition produce effects of dynamic movement, whereas rectilinear ones tend to be calmer and more static.

■ The diagonal is the longest dimension in a garden plot – exploiting this line makes for the longest vista.

■ Diagonal lines can be devised to deflect the gaze away from an eyesore.

■ Often, existing features can be the jumping-off point for a diagonal composition – such as the position of an existing gate, shed, greenhouse, or garage.

Creating movement across a space
Zigzag layouts of paths or planting, (such as low hedges of lavender or box) create movement across a space, and especially as here, where an arch of roses has been introduced, make for a progression through a series of separate and different planting areas.

access and for visual effect (opening up new views to the space beyond). Remember to keep secret areas that can be glimpsed but not fully seen in order to create a sense that the garden extends far beyond its real boundaries. As Alexander Pope wrote in the early 18th century: "Let not each beauty everywhere be spied, when half the skill is decently to hide." Gardens benefit from a feeling of expectation and surprise.

A tapered space also has possibilities in the manipulation of false perspective, providing in a small compass a vanishing point that can be used to create the illusion of greater depth than actually exists. In this respect there are several tricks that can be deployed. Diminishing, tapered lines in paving, though less easy to lay than parallel slabs, have a surprisingly lengthening effect on a short path. Alternatively, making a diagonal path with a zigzag direction increases the interest and creates more dynamism within the design. Or again, try laying out a path in decking with a change of direction in the way the boarding is positioned.

Strong diagonal emphasis need not be confined to paths or hard-landscaping: it can be devised by the way diagonal bed edges are treated. For example, a planting of box, *Teucrium chamaedrys*, lavender, or *Ophiophogon nigrescens* around the edge of a bed or border would contrast strongly in colour and texture with a less formal planting within the bed, and would make a strong statement in a garden of any size. In a similar way, the bold drifts of grasses and herbaceous perennials favoured by Piet Oudolf can be planted with a sufficiently confident sweep to make a new direction in an informal garden entirely of plants as opposed to a structure. Whatever the method selected, it is important to stick to simple, bold lines – and not too many of them.

▲ **Garden of diagonals**
This garden has been entirely laid out on diagonals. The main cross paths are set at the same angle as the cross on the St Andrew's flag. This makes for dynamic vistas in all directions. The two pools are lozenge shaped, to echo the layout. The raised beds and the trellis screens, all set at the same angles as the paths, create perspectives that project the ground plan into three dimensions.

▶ **Contrasts in light and dark**
Light-coloured stone edging has been used to divide beds from grass, and the strong saw-tooth pattern that this produces imbues a sense of dynamic movement into what was originally a static, oblong space. The sharp colour contrast of the stone against green helps reinforce the effect.

▲ All at an angle

This bird's eye view shows clearly that all the hard landscaping – steps, pergola, and terrace – have been laid diagonally across this walled, oblong plot. The triangular beds thus created "read" as such from above, yet their shape is less easy to discern at ground level.

◄ Visual guidelines

Very few bold lines are enough to suggest a directional movement across a garden. In this case, irregularly lengthed paving slabs set into gravel give an emphasis to the garden that ignores its real shape and makes the most of its diagonal, and therefore longest, dimension.

▼ Triangles within rectangles

Setting out a deck on the diagonal creates planting pockets that help confuse the rectangular plan of the plot. It also tends to maximize the visual space, since the vistas use the longer, diagonal dimension. This compositional device is carried through in the positioning of pots and furniture in the garden.

Garden rooms of different character

Even very small gardens can benefit from being subdivided into separate outdoor "rooms". This can both increase the apparent size and offer an opportunity to develop planting of differing styles.

Many of us have become familiar with the notion of subdividing gardens into separate, clearly defined sections via the inspiring examples at Sissinghurst Castle Garden in Kent and Hidcote Manor Garden in Gloucestershire, but it is not always appreciated that the idea need not be confined to gardens on a grand scale. It is a paradox that the subdivision of limited garden space, either by hedge, screen, or change of surface, can make the plot appear larger. Sometimes a much less formal subdivision than a hedge or wall will have the same effect: for example, a dense bank of evergreen shrubs. This visual trick works for a variety of reasons. Firstly, the true extent of the site may be hidden; secondly, the eye is distracted by the increase in the variety of planting and effect; and, thirdly, there is an extra element of expectation and surprise created by the nooks and crannies of a diversified layout.

The very common long, thin shape of many urban and suburban plots lends itself particularly well to this idea. Imagine a series of partially screened compartments along the length of such a space, visually and actually linked by either a straight or serpentine path. Depending on the length available, you might be able to create four or five different areas that could comprise – in order leading from the house – a terrace and open lawn, a contained flower garden, a vegetable plot, a drying ground or play space, and finally a well-

Why create subdivisions?

■ It is unexpectedly true that subdividing even the smallest garden space can make it seem larger.

■ In long, thin gardens, create a series of "rooms" of different character and function and divide them by hedges or trellis screens.

■ A partitioned garden works equally well with formal or informal divisions.

■ Subdivisions hide the true extent of a garden and create a sense of expectation and surprise.

◄ **Visual compartments**
Garden "rooms" may be implied rather than physically subdivided, so think of ways of suggesting divisions that separate areas without solid walls. Such visual full stops can create distinct sections of quite different character while retaining views between one and the another.

► **Changes in mood**
The division of a garden into separate rooms enables you to include sections in quite different styles. Here a very simple, formal "dining-room" – defined only by yew hedging – is juxtaposed against an area of more complex, informal planting.

▲ Insubstantial "walls"
The divisions of a garden room can be insiginficant, as here, where a light screen of welded-steel mesh has been used to define one "wall" of an outdoor dining-room. The other "walls" are only suggested by posts, by box balls and box edging, and by the paving on which the table and chairs sit.

▼ Marking a garden area
Outdoor rooms don't have to have walls: they can be defined by changes of surface, or by the loosest divisions at ground level. However, there should be well-defined entrances and exits, which demarcate a change of style and character. Here, breaks in a low wall and a flight of steps fulfil this function.

► Using similar materials
A clearly defined link between an indoor and an outdoor area can be effective. In some cases, however, the division between the two may be so inconspicuous that it is hard to distinguish whether you are sitting indoors or out. This use of decking visually extends the conservatory/dining-room into the garden.

screened area for storage, compost, and so on. A site 8m (25ft) wide x 15m (50ft) long would be sufficient to achieve this ambitious list, while smaller areas could fit two or three compartments.

One obvious way of achieving the subdivisions is to use evergreen or deciduous hedges to a height of 1.5–1.8m (5–6ft). They work particularly well when defining formal areas such as outdoor dining-rooms and sitting areas, but can often be too shady in a confined space if you are trying to achieve a self-contained herbaceous or rose garden, a potager, or straightforward herb or vegetable beds. For these purposes, a lighter, more open screen of trellis works well, or a lower planting of box, *Santolina* or lavender.

Changes in ground surface are as important a method as vertical divisions in defining distinct areas. You could use, for example, the crisp edges of decking to divide and distinguish banks of informal planting. Alternatively, a change of surface as you move from one space to the next can help define the character of each compartment in the garden.

Instead of formal divisions, you could have a loose screen of bamboo or a thicket of hardy palms and tree ferns. This will create a feeling of jungle that would, for example, contrast nicely with the light and airy feel of a well-kept lawn. In fact, when devising outdoor rooms, you should bear in mind that maximum contrast in

Garden rooms of different character 33

◄ **Change of mood**
A very simple change of
ground surface from grass
to a chequerboard of grass
alternating with paving slabs
alters the character of a hedged
room completely. Gardens rooms
benefit from maximum contrast:
light to dark; or simple to
complex. All gardens need areas
of extreme simplicity to give
counterpoint to areas of rich,
jewel-like intricacy.

► **Town garden cleverly
subdivided into sections**
The foreground terrace is
separated from a sunk pool
garden by a bed of architectural
foliage backed by a yew hedge.
Beyond the far yew hedge is a
wild area planted with several
species of rampant bamboo.
The movement from one space
to the next is made more
interesting by the change from a
central path in the foreground to
a split, double path farther back.

◄ **Enticing vista**
This garden exploits bold scale as
well as the simplest of sculptural
forms to achieve a progression
through different spaces. Here
the all-green planting relies on
changes of texture and shade
for its interest. The hole in the
circular stone sculpture suggests
further space beyond it.

style, colour, and texture as you move from area to area can produce
the best effect. It is the same charm of diversity that is often
experienced when looking from an upper window at a row of urban
gardens, all by accident different in style – some simple, some
complicated, the one making a pleasing foil for its neighbour. So
many of these streetscapes make you realize how many-faceted are
tastes in gardening and how effective quite radical jumps in style
can be. Like a meal, all gardens need a juxtaposition of simplicity
against complexity so that they do not become visually indigestible.
In laying out even the tiniest plot, plan for some simple areas: mown
grass, or a flat drift of the same plant or plain paving. These will set
off areas of complex, colourful, or detailed planting.

▲ Wooden patterns
Different types of fencing suggest divisions, which are further defined by contrasting light and shade. Simple, openwork trellis and palings look well silhouetted against lighter planting so that their patterns can be more easily appreciated.

◄ Changes of planting style
Variations in planting can be as effective a visual device as a wall or hedge in creating a well-defined separate area of garden. Here, informal, bold groups including *Ligularia* 'The Rocket', *Aruncus dioicus*, and *Cornus alba* make a complex foreground to much simpler compositions in the distance.

Gardens on different levels

A flat site may be the easiest to deal with but it lacks the interest of one with level changes; this, however, can readily be remedied. Basement areas and steep slopes also offer scope for exciting effects.

Steps, ramps, and small paved platforms will diversify a level site and can help define a place to sit or an area for an urn or other object.

A series of shallow, sloping steps – perhaps forming the treads in mown grass and the shallow risers in brick or stone bands – is one of the simplest and most effective devices for a gentle slope rising away from a house. These look particularly well when they occupy more-or-less the full width of the garden. Devise the raised masonary bands so that they make mowing easy, as in the example on the right.

A slope running away from the house requires rather different treatment since it will be less visible. Think of turning such a declivity into a series of terraces with retaining walls, or a series of broad levels with steeper banks, rather than a continuous or slightly broken slope. The artificially produced flat areas will be those that are visible, and these might be planted to advantage with a series of verticals such as pencil cypresses or fastigiated junipers, which will emphasize the level changes and remain visible when looking both up and down the scene.

Where, as often happens, a slope runs in two directions, more ingenuity is required to devise a plan. A starting-off point will be that at least a small, level terrace or lawn ought to be included – a garden that is all slope is generally unsatisfactory – you need at least a small space to sit. The precise position of this flat area in relation to the house will usually become apparent from the topography but it should not be too distant from the house itself. The greatest help in planning the layout will be a site survey showing existing levels. This can be commissioned from a surveyor and will be invaluable in designing steps and the "cut-and-fill" operations necessary to create different levels and ramps.

Methods of retaining slopes are many and varied – stone or brick walls being perhaps the most common. However, there are many simpler solutions such as substantial timber sleepers or new,

◄ Sloping gardens
Substantial level changes will often need an architectural solution such as the construction of steps and retaining walls to create drama and offer the opportunity to introduce a mixture of hard landscaping materials that are interesting in themselves. Steps, walls, and paving will need the softening effect of planting.

▲ Making a garden look wide
Broad, shallow steps of grass with stone risers make a grand approach to a raised terrace. The horizontal lines of the ramped steps are echoed by the long, low pergola and bench. Such a layout filling the full width of a narrow town garden would give it a very spacious feel.

Why different levels?

■ Changes of level add drama and interest to a garden – they either make the most of a sloping site or introduce artificial breaks of levels in a flat one.

■ A garden that is all slope is generally unsatisfactory. Create at least small level areas that give you somewhere to sit – such areas will also emphasize the slopes or steps.

■ A slope running away from a house requires different treatment to one that rises from it.

■ Consider the many different methods available to build steps – from the very informal grass treads with wood risers to formal, fully dressed stone.

■ In a small garden, including steps to the full width of the site will engender a sense of grandeur.

▲ **Upper-level terrace**
Where there is a rise away from a house, it may be
better to site the sitting area well away from the
house rather than in the more usual position leading
straight from the main rooms. However, the exact
location should depend on where the sun shines.

pressure-treated, stout planks. The wattle hurdles used to make raised turf seats in the Middle Ages are also a possibility and can be especially effective in creating curved retaining walls – a job for which they are well adapted.

Though the dimensions of all steps are, of course, to some extent determined by the space available and the height to be scaled, any time spent in careful planning will prove extremely worthwhile. A good rule is to keep steps simple, straight, and rectilinear – small, curved steps are almost always a mistake. It is generally effective to go for low risers, not more than 15cm (6in) high, and deep treads, with 40cm (16in) or more from front to back. Broad and spacious landings where there are changes in direction are much more satisfactory than small ones. Generous proportions in steps and landings apply equally to small and to large spaces, and they will considerably improve the scale of a small site even if they more or less fill it.

You should also consider the many methods available to build steps. For an informal setting the simplicity of timber posts supporting timber board risers with grass, gravel, or bark treads are appropriate and cheap to construct. In a more formal setting, brick risers with stone treads are a good choice.

To achieve a successful, curved staircase you need plenty of space and generous curves, though on a grand scale nothing is more charming than a flight of concave steps followed by a convex run with a broad landing between them. This theatrical arrangement could be achieved on a small, sloping site if it occupied most or all of the available space and would make a great staging for the display of plants in pots.

▶ Changes in height
Even very slight alterations in level add interest to a garden. Here two steps and a low, brick retaining wall divide a small garden into separate areas. Raising the central pot by one brick with a stone capping is sufficient to continue the idea, even though the rest of the garden is flat. Small, artificial changes in the contour of paving can have a disproportionately large impact on the look of the garden.

Variety of retaining materials
This vegetable and herb garden illustrates some of the many materials that are available for retaining changes of level – in this instance stone, timber, and wattle. Woven wattle like this was used in the Middle Ages to retain turf seats, which were in effect raised beds with turf tops. These varied materials add interest and texture to the garden in winter, when there is little foliage.

Walls, Fences, & Hedges

Enlivening the garden's boundaries

Receding screens

One of the ways to add depth and perspective to a garden is to impose onto the main viewpoint a series of paired screens, one behind the other, using the principles of theatrical stage scenery.

The screens can be formed of hedging, trellis. or informal blocks of planting. Such a simple framing device adds immeasurably to the spatial interest of a garden.

The illusion of depth in the theatre is achieved by introducing a series of painted canvas "flats" positioned one behind the other, maybe of diminishing height, and perhaps increasingly close together. On the stage, the "flats" might be of painted canvas representing staffage – a dark framing device, usually of trees. The same basic system can be adopted in gardens by employing pairs of flanking hedges, trellis screens clothed with climbers, or even darkly coloured informal planting.

This method of framing the main view of a garden works particularly well in a typical urban plot with a long, thin shape. Think of the garden as a stage set with the proscenium at the main windows of the house. The central vista would be the backcloth of the stage set, with the flanking screens the "flats", and the spaces between them the "wings" of the stage. These "wings" or recesses between the "flats" become separate gardens where different types of planting can be visually isolated from each other.

The simplest way of framing a viewpoint is to arrange six trellis panels in pairs right up to the left and right boundary of the site. The first pair should be at least 1.8–2.4m (6–8ft) tall and no wider than

Why receding screens?

- Take a cue from the theatre by arranging your garden as if it were viewed through the proscenium of a stage.

- Use the idea of theatrical "flats" to increase the sense of depth in the garden. They can be of trellis, hedging, or informal planting.

- The flanking screens enhance the illusionary perspective if they become closer together the farther they are from the viewer.

- Arrange the screens so that the darkest is in the foreground with the lightest at the back.

- Use the space between the screens for planting schemes that will be visually insulated from each other.

 **Subdividing with trellis**
Give depth to a garden by introducing a series of vertical layers. These can consist of a variety of materials: trellis (as shown here), hedges, or substantial blocks of planting. The idea is to provide a sense of progression through the garden.

▶ **Tricking the eye**
The geometry of bold, half-lapped trellis forms a foil for a lush planting of *Alchemilla mollis*, astrantia, *Trachystemon orientalis*, and standard bays. This planting layer effectively provides a middle ground within the garden scene, turning the summerhouse into a notionally distant viewstopper.

▲ Integrated design
The basic compositional device of foreground, middle ground, and distance can be made up of the simplest elements. Here hornbeam hedges (the middle ground) frame, like stage scenery, the view of a distant hornbeam hedge, which has a niche cut into it housing an urn. The foreground is provided by low trellis-fenced beds of lavender out of which rise mopheads of Portugal laurel.

▶ Theatrical design
This garden relies on perspective to create an illusion of space – it is in fact only 5m (15ft) wide. Dark green trellis-encased yews separated by light-coloured gravel paths provide a dark frame for pale grey columns flanking foil-backed glass.

90cm (3ft). The length of the garden will determine how far behind the next pair is placed, but make sure that the spacing between the first pair and the second is greater than between the last pair. Each pair should be increasingly shorter and wider – the second maybe 1.5–2.1m (5–7ft) high x 1.2m (4ft) wide, the third 1.2–1.8m (4–6ft) high x 1.5m (5ft) wide. The last pair of screens should be some distance in front of the back fence or wall, and this back perimeter should be covered in a matching trellis, which spans the full width of the site and is a little lower than the last pair of screens.

Support the freestanding screens on substantial timber posts of at least 10 x 10cm (4 x 4in). Colour the trellis to make a contrast with foliage so that their structure will still "read" when they are planted with climbers or have other planting in front and behind them. Good colours would be dark blackish green, blue-grey, white, black, or grey – in fact, architectural as opposed to natural colours.

The same design principles apply if hedges or informal planting clumps are used. Indeed hedges can be planted alongside trellis, so that the trellis gives the effect while the hedge is growing up behind it, and at the same time acts as a guide for its clipping. Suitable hedging plants are dark evergreens such as yew and holly, *Quercus ilex*, *Phillyrea latifolia*, or pyracantha. The last is particularly effective in a confined space since it can be trained against trellis as an espalier and kept much thinner than conventional hedging plants. All these look good if they are cut in sharply geometric shapes. However, groups of less-defined, dark trees and shrubs can be used in a similar way, though they require more space. Make sure there is sufficient definition between the groups by spacing them adequately and making the greens of each group distinctly different. The same grading of height and width applies as before. Make sure that the darkest coloured groups are in the foreground.

Hidden spaces
The visual complexity of this roof terrace, made up of a forest of trellis columns, means that it impossible to determine how big it really is. The nooks and crannies between the columns hint at further space beyond. The height of the closely spaced vertical laths ensure privacy.

Hiding unpleasant objects

Every garden has its unattractive elements, and usually there are views outside the garden that you might wish were not there. Demolition or removal, however, is not often an option.

There are various ways to conceal or mitigate the effect of horrible visual intrusions, however large they are. For example, you may need to think laterally – as in the case of the tower block on p.56 – by effectively cutting off the views towards the eyesore.

You should pinpoint the prime points to be avoided and plan the garden from the start to minimize them. The following are some of the first things to consider when drawing up your plans. Is the garden overlooked badly by neighbour's windows? Can the effect of a five-storey blank wall (not your own) be improved? Can oil tanks, swimming-pool equipment, dustbins, cars, the detritus of a working garden area, or neighbour's shed be hidden? The answer, with some ingenuity, is usually "yes".

If concealment is out of the question, try introducing a distraction by leading the eye in another direction or making such a compelling eye-catcher that you fail to notice what at first seemed startlingly and unpleasantly obvious.

Perhaps the simplest, if not the quickest, solution is to "plant out" the offending object with strategically placed trees, hedges, or shrubs. In this context, evergreens are invaluable since they provide year-round camouflage. Suitable quick-growing and controllable plants are yew, cherry laurel, Portugal laurel, *Quercus ilex*, and *Phillyrea latifolia*. Do not necessarily plant them as close to the object to be hidden as possible – a tree or shrubbery in the foreground provides more visual cover than one farther back.

▶ **Making a virtue from a necessity**
The staircase into this dark basement garden could have been an eyesore, but instead it forms an integral part of the design – its positive rather than its negative features being highlighted. It has been lit to cast dramatic shadows against white walls and has been painted to tone with the grey-and-green colour scheme. A small canal below it reflects light through the open treads.

◀ **Offending objects**
The whole layout of the garden should be designed to distract attention away from an eyesore. Subterfuges such as the principal paths leading to a viewstopper, as here, will help the eye focus somewhere else.

▶ **Clever disguise**
A lean-to shed has been transformed by two new facades very simply made of stained shuttering ply and sawn timber. They hide a boring roof line behind baroque gables. The applied trellis gives texture to the plain surface of ply.

Coping with unpleasant objects

■ Careful planning at the earliest stage can conceal even the most distressingly large eyesore.

■ If the object to be hidden is too large or prominent to be physically concealed, introduce a distraction: provide, for example, a large object in the foreground that demands attention from the viewer.

■ Brightly coloured objects tend to jump forwards visually, while cooler, paler-coloured ones tend to recede.

■ Take inspiration from military camouflage: a well-placed piece of foliage will break up the most solid block of masonry.

■ Don't tolerate a nasty-looking garden shed – turn it into a pleasing eye-catcher or a folly.

▼ Dramatic viewstopper
This useful screen would be excellent for concealing a neighbour's eyesore. Adjust the scale of such a feature to hide whatever needs camouflage. In this case a background of bamboo and strong lighting make anything beyond seem insignificant at night.

▶ Hiding a utility area
Willow fencing has been used to screen the working department of a garden: greenhouse, pots, tools, compost, and hoses. This sort of self-contained garden within a garden can be devised in even the smallest site. The simple, block-like effect makes a good foil for planting and should be left, as here, undecorated and unplanted.

◀ Seeing double
Only one of these square sheds hides a tank – the other was built for the sake of symmetry. Pairs of garden buildings are particularly useful: they can frame a vista if sited in the foreground, or hide two sets of neighbours at the end of a garden.

You may need to provide plant screening from several viewpoints. A good way to work out size and position is to hold up sheets of thin ply and judge their screening effect from several sightlines. It is also important that such quick-growing planting does not get out of control., because it will very soon take over the whole garden unless it is annually assessed and pruned accordingly.

Screening of a more architectural kind needs to be attractive in itself as well as fitting in with the design of the rest of the garden. Think of colour-coordinating fence panels with other woodwork or garden buildings and don't colour them too luridly if their function is to help conceal something behind them. A freestanding enclosure made of wattle hurdle or stained vertical boarding, for example, can make an attractive object in itself (see above), and could contain all the messy workings of a garden.

A properly placed, attractively designed garden shed also has great screening potential. Even the plainest, off-the-peg shed can be re-coloured or customized with a new façade of interesting outline, or it can be clad with timber-backed trellis to provide a support for climbers. Think of making the shed into a kind of folly or eye-catcher that would make a good termination to the garden scene as well as providing cover. It is usually not difficult to move an existing shed to a more effective position for camouflage purposes.

◄▼ Towering eyesore
A larger, more intractable blot on the landscape would be hard to invent than this tower block, but its impact on the view from a nearby garden has been reduced to almost zero by inventive use of overhead planting and perimeter screening. Inside the garden, a lightly constructed pergola spans the whole space, acting in effect as a series of planted overhead louvres that block the view upwards. The lower floors of the building are hidden by a perimeter wall heightened by horizontal trellis.

► Privacy curtain
High panels of punched stainless-steel sheeting create a screen against tall overlooking buildings yet admit light. Because of their shiny surface and carefully detailed minimalist design, without visible framing or support, they have an airy, insubstantial appearance.

Adding height to a screen wall

An existing fence or wall may not be high enough for privacy or to mask the surroundings to your garden, so why not extend the height and at the same time neaten or green up the perimeter.

Such an extension will also make a better backdrop for the main elements of the garden design. How you raise a perimeter boundary may depend on the date your house was built, and the material used in the existing perimeter boundary fence. An 18th- or 19th-century house will probably have a brick wall – generally, less than 1.8m (6ft) high. A 20th- or 21st-century house is more likely to have a timber or link-mesh fence – more than likely, this is unsightly in itself and probably affords little privacy from neighbours and surrounding buildings.

You should first decide whether you want a solid extension to the screen wall (maybe close boarding, an evergreen hedge, or a climber); an openwork effect (trellis or carefully trained pleached trees, for example); or a translucent screen (which will let light through while obscuring the view). Each will require different materials and approaches to the problem. You also need to consider the original wall or fence height. In a formal scheme think of extending the height perhaps in more than one layer – an extension of trellis actually sitting on top of the wall with a pleached or pollarded hedge slightly in front of the wall. This gives a small slot for light where the trellis is exposed below the canopy of the stilt; it also varies the texture and colour of the boundary itself.

The easiest way to raise a low (1–1.2m/3–4ft) wall or boarded fence is to fix into the ground, or bolt to the wall, some 7.5 x 7.5cm (3 x 3in) or 10 x 10cm (4 x 4in) timber posts of the required new

◄ Increasing privacy at a boundary
Where a wall or fence is too low to provide the required screening, or a real sense of enclosure, you can add height to it using trellis, planting such as a pleached hedge, or a combination of the two. A screen of 1.8–2.4m (6–8ft) gives enough protection in most situations.

Boundary screens

■ Extra height or bulk can be added to any kind of wall or fence – be it brick, timber, open metal netting, or trellis – that may be too low to hide a neighbour's garden or to give satisfactory shelter.

■ Think of increasing the height with planting or timber extensions, or a combination of the two.

■ One of the most common methods is to raise the height of a wall with a trellis extension that is fixed to it – this can be kept open or can be planted up, rendering it virtually impenetrable.

■ A stilt hedge of pleached or pollarded lime or hornbeam, planted just in front of a wall or fence, makes a green band of foliage above it and helps formalize or "green up" a plot.

◄ **Trellis above a wall**
An easy way to extend the height of a wall to give partial screening without cutting out sunlight. These off-the-peg panels of diagonal trellis are fixed between posts that could be either plugged to the wall or set into the ground. The top of the panels have been capped by a weather-protective moulding. Use stained, pressure-treated timber for longest life.

◄ Doubling the height of a boundary
These pleached hornbeams are twice as tall as the low wall behind them. If they are trained and cut with care, it will still be possible for light to pass through them and for partial through-views to be enjoyed. Train the laterals, as here, on bamboo canes or on strained wires between strong, metal uprights.

► Different ways to fix trellis
A white-painted brick wall is here extended in height by horizontal trellis using two methods: on the left, the trellis is raised on posts screwed to the wall; on the right, it is secured at full height between posts set into the ground a little in front of the rear wall. The gap allows plenty of space for climbers on both sides of the screen.

height, spaced at not more than 1.8m (6ft) intervals. They will provide the fixings for close boarding or trellis panels, which can be positioned on top of the wall if it is fixed to your neighbour's side of the posts, or can go from ground level to the new full height if secured to your side of the posts.

One colour almost always best avoided for such wooden extensions is the most common standard colour for timber fencing – the bright orange-brown of much pressure-treated timber or the similarly coloured stain used as standard on boarded or woven fencing or sheds. This colour is unsuitable for a boundary that you want to lose visually since it is a jumping-forward colour and is difficult to disguise. Choose a much more muted blue-grey, grey, dark green, or black – all of which tend to "disappear". This colouring can be applied as an opaque paint onto already stained timber or as a stain on clear, pressure-treated timber (the latter being the best to ask for when ordering new timber fencing).

Another method of adding height to an existing fence is to cover the whole surface in a simple trellis taller than fence panels but in the same panel widths – this enables the existing posts to be used, thereby drawing attention to the panels and dividing up the run. In most circumstances it will be better to keep the trellis and the panel colour the same, so the effect is not too busy. Allow climbers or other plants to provide the interest. In the case of an open-link fence, consider planting with a thin-growing but rigid wall shrub such as *Pyracantha coccinea*, which will both give substance to the fence and can be used to raise its height by 30–60cm (1–2ft).

A particularly attractive way to cloth a perimeter with openwork foliage is to plant a series of pleached or espaliered trees at intervals as close to the fence or wall as possible – bearing in mind that a wall will have foundations protruding (usually by not more than 23cm/9in). Suitable subjects for pleaching or espaliers are lime (*Tilia* spp.) and hornbeam (*Carpinus betulus*), *Pyracantha coccinea*, apple, and pear. Most, with the exception of lime, need support in the form of horizontal training wires or timber laths in the early stages, though when the plants are mature they become self-supporting. Such openwork foliage requires diligent annual pruning to keep it in shape. The key to a successful effect with pleaching and pollards is always to be on top of pruning during the growing season and in autumn – in the first years clipping and tying in 2–3 times a year or as necessary. However pleaching and pollards are definitely worth the effort and give a delightful green geometry to the garden, and act as a good foil to informal planting.

▼ Steel-backed trellis
The whole perimeter of this tiny garden has been clad with trellis backed by galvanized-steel sheeting. The steel is not quite to the top of the 1.8m (6ft) high trellis panels. Instead of visible posts, the trellis is supported by broad, 30cm (1ft) wide pilasters of galvanized steel, which conceal pairs of posts.

► Roof-top protection
Wind screening is particularly important on exposed roof terraces, and these translucent glass panels on stainless-steel supports give protection without cutting out too much light. Roof gardens need tough plants such as bamboo, which here softens the effect of hard perimeter surfaces. A mix of natural and machine-made materials adds further variety to what might otherwise be an arid environment.

Unifying the house and boundary

The alterations and messy rebuilds that many houses suffer from can be rectified and improved by gardening and garden-related activities rather more easily and cheaply than by building works.

Very often the garden side of a town house, particularly in the case of 19th- and early 20th-century terrace houses, has little or no regularity – all the design consistency has been put into the grander and more symmetrical street elevation. Kitchen and scullery extensions leave awkward, dark, and cramped corners surrounded by building on three sides. You need to think of ways of colonizing these difficult spaces by making them feel part of the garden, greening them up and looking less drab, and, at the same time, giving them some design consistency.

One way to unify a messy elevation or series of elevations – not just of the house but of all the garden boundaries – is to clad all faces in a consistently detailed, simple trellis. The visual unity that this gives tends to distract attention from unsightly windows of differing and uncoordinated design, downpipes, vents, and so on.

When you cover all the walls of the house that face the garden to just above window height, the strong horizontal line formed by the capping of the trellis (which should be more substantial in section than the trellis itself) will tend to neaten up windows of different heights, shapes, and types. Clothe the trellis with free-growing climbers or wall shrubs and you further fudge the messy architecture, completely hiding pipework, vents, drains, as well as softening the perimeter of window openings.

Surface improvements

■ Very few houses have perfectly proportioned garden boundaries, and most are surrounded by an odd assortment of walls or fences. Think of regularizing them using paint, consistent planting of climbers or wall shrubs, or new cladding.

■ Cladding a house wall with trellis gives an instant face-lift to a building. Fit it up to ground-floor ceiling height, carefully placing it round windows and doors.

■ Paint unattractive windows and doors with a dark colour or one close to the colour of the wall in which they are set.

■ Run the perimeter treatment of a garden consistently round all sides and continue in modified form across the garden faces of the house.

◄ **Treating a house and its garden setting in a unified way**
This is a rare example of a house with a garden façade that is regular and relates to the rest of the garden. The universal application of a coordinated surface, such as trellis, here offset by pilasters, helps in this respect. Tall perimeter treatments may need planning permission.

▶ **Leafy cover-up**
A random collection of windows, drainpipes, and irregularly shaped walls has been disguised by the application of large-scale trellis planted with climbers – *Clematis* and *Trachelospermum jasminoides*. A hornbeam column on the right conceals a recess and a tangle of plumbing.

◀ **Oriental style**
Split-cane shading makes a good screen attached to a stout bamboo frame. Such materials are particularly appropriate to oriental-style planting such as the "cloud"-clipped *Ilex crenata* seen here. The effect of such fencing relies on extreme neatness.

◀ **Screens from the East**
This plastered and painted wall, framed by black timber, shows an alternative oriental-style screen. The same effect could be achieved by white-painted ply panels set within timber studwork painted a different colour. Such very simple backgrounds make the ideal foil for free-growing conifers and gnarled rockwork.

▶ **Bamboo background**
A different form of split-cane screening – one designed for greenhouse shading – makes a lovely background to varied foliage such as wisteria, acer, and eucalyptus. Hang the screen over unattractive fencing or disparate wall surfaces, but make sure it is carefully levelled and lined up.

Suitable climbing plants for this sort of setting, often in dark and shady positions, are *Holboellia cociacea*, *Trachelospermum jasminoides*, the evergreen honeysuckle *Lonicera japonica*, *Hydrangea petiolaris*, and the many interesting climbing ivies. Of course a mixture of climbers will give a longer flowering season. Early flowering *Clematis cirrhosa* (January and February flowering) and *C. armandii* (March to April flowering) could be planted against climbing roses, hops, and wisteria to achieve this.

Another way to create a strong unifying effect is by applying the same paint colour to the ground-floor walls of the house, to the garden walls and fences, and to garden buildings and structures. This works particularly well if the surfaces to be painted can be made relatively consistent: for example, by using rendered masonry with adjacent timber fences covered in smooth-painted ply to resemble render.

Think of other inventive ways of making the surfaces of house, fences, and so on consistent. The continuous planting of a clipped wall shrub such as *Pyracantha coccinea*, *Phillyrea latifolia*, or *Rhamnus alaternus* can be kept tight to a wall or fence and will, with diligent pruning, remain relatively thin. Pyracantha is still seen beautifully espaliered on the walls of cottages, while both phillyrea and *Rhamnus alaternus* were commonly used as trained wall shrubs in the 17th and 18th centuries. Like all wall planting, these will require a well-prepared site as close as possible to the wall or fence.

Other materials, or combinations of materials, that may provide a uniform surface include wattle hurdles, galvanized welded mesh, and bamboo screening. The main points to bear in mind are the need to cap the cladding to a consistent height with boldly sized capping – perhaps just 10 x 5cm (4 x 2in) sawn timber painted or stained a matching colour, and to pay particular attention to the edge treatment around openings – doors, windows, gates, and so on. They need to be neatly edged to give visual substance to the cladding material – perhaps a simple square-section timber architrave matching the capping will be sufficient. It may be that these openings in the cladding should themselves be consistent in shape and size, as far as possible.

Differently styled window frames and glazed doors can be effectively camouflaged by painting their frames as close as possible to the colour of the wall or new cladding, or by painting them a dark colour so that in daylight they hardly "read" visually at all. The one colour that should be avoided when painting door and window frames is that orange-red stain which seeks to imitate wood, but which neither recedes nor makes a satisfactory contrast with glazing. Instead, choose architectural colours, rather than bright or lurid, strong ones. White, off-white, or light stone colours will emphasize an attractively shaped window, while black, dark green, or dark grey will play down an unsatisfactory one or minimize the effect of random openings in a wall.

Coordinated setting
The charming effect of backlighting on reed screening emphasizes its light, elegant profile. The horizontal emphasis of the reeds is cleverly picked up in the grooves of the decking and the slats of the furniture. This tiny enclosed space has its own character entirely independent of its surroundings.

Dissolving the perimeter

If you cannot see the edges of your plot, it is difficult for the eye to gauge where the boundary actually is and consequently the size of the garden could be limitless.

Obfuscation is the name of the game when trying to conceal the real geometric boundary that most sites have. For example, a bold, serpentine-shaped planting of trees and shrubs will break up the line of a fence. This informal method requires that plants are positioned forwards in some places, and further back in others so they recede almost back to the line of the perimeter. A contrast in texture and shades of green works better than the use of bold colours when providing the visual complexity needed to "dissolve" a boundary. Reserve strong colours for the foreground of your scene, and keep the perimeter background in monochromatic greens so that it does not draw attention to itself. There are so many delightful shades and textures available that an all-green composition of plants will certainly not be boring.

Take care to vary the planting heights as well as depths. You should try to break the line of the boundary in every way, and variation in height is essential to cut into the horizontal line of a fence or wall. You should also think of "using" planting in a

neighbour's garden – incorporating into the plan, if possible, trees and shrubs so that they relate to your own planting scheme and seem part of it. In the 18th century, this would have been termed "borrowed landscape" – that is, taking advantage of scenery that you do not own. Even quite distant trees can be annexed, as it were, by being framed or otherwise drawn into the scene.

In recent years, the classic way of dissolving a garden boundary has been to introduce outdoor mirrors. This can be very effective in small town gardens, especially on the back wall or fence facing the principal view. To gain maximum effect, mirrors must be positioned as far away from the viewer as possible – this will usually be on or near the actual boundary of the garden. A mirror in a strategic position on the boundary reflects your own garden into the space beyond it. Slight changes in the angle at which the mirror is set make a big difference to what they reflect. An upwards angle will show the sky, and a side angle may reflect foliage more satisfactorily than a straight-on position. A key trick is to hide the edges of the

◄ Soft edges
This planting scheme ignores the boundary and thus conceals the true extent of the garden. It doesn't matter that plants encroach into usable, open area; the varied outline creates a sense of indeterminate space that might be much larger than can be appreciated at a glance.

▲ Disguised limits
It is hard to discern the real shape of this garden. The actual boundary is well concealed behind a series of planting layers at various levels and positions. A dummy screen formed by the stems of standard *Ligustrum lucidum* marks a notional boundary that is backed by a dark screen of evergreens.

How to "lose" boundary edges

■ Conceal the real geometric boundary of the garden with a boldly indented, informal planting of trees and shrubs that breaks up the horizontal lines of hedges, walls, and fences.

■ Use a mirror to fool the eye into thinking the garden goes on beyond its boundary.

■ Make the presence of the mirror hard to detect by hiding its edges with foliage.

■ Galvanized sheeting fixed to a boundary – and perhaps fronted with trellis – gives an insubstantial, airy feel to the perimeter without the disconcerting effect of precise reflections.

■ Consider "borrowing" some of the surrounding landscape by visually incorporating a neighbour's plants into your own scheme.

▲ Maximizing the visual space
Three mirrors with broad architrave frames dissolve one boundary of this garden. The softening of their edges with planting is key to the visual illusion, making it difficult to see where the glass begins and ends.

▼ Secluded setting
This delightfully eccentric interpretation of the Gothick in fencing provides support for a tall, exuberant planting of roses, lavatera, and weeds. This design enables the boundary of a tiny, cottage front garden to be virtually hidden. Even though the garden is close to a road, from inside the house it might be in rustic isolation.

► Multi-layered planting
A series of planting levels of varied height and character give the illusion of wilderness, distracting the viewer from thoughts of boundaries or containment. The precisely clipped forms of box and *Liguistrum delavayanum* are essential counterpoints. Without these, the garden would be a mess of unstructured foliage.

mirror with an irregular line of foliage so that you aren't sure where reality begins and reflection ends. Openwork gates backed by mirror glass give the illusion that the garden continues beyond the perceived plot – and again the gate itself hides the presence of mirror. Only on-site experiment, however, will give you the best option for mirror positions.

The illusions of reflection have become especially popular with the advent of cheap plastic substitutes for mirror glass. Acrylic and polystyrene mirrors make weatherproof and cheap alternatives to glass, and are available in large, uninterrupted sheets up to

2.4 x 1.2m (8 x 4ft) as standard. Alternatively think of using reflective materials that do not have a sharp, mirror-like image. They have the advantage of not containing precise images, and they do not double the apparent number of people in the garden. Galvanized-steel sheet has just this quality: it reflects light and the general shape of what it faces, without the disturbing effect of precise reflection. This material tends to give the illusion that there is no barrier at all – especially, again, when used with trellis in front of it. Its vague reflective qualities have the effect of dissolving the boundary quite as convincingly as mirror glass.

Tricks of the light
The indefinite reflection of galvanized steel behind grey-stained trellis visually distances the boundary of this highly controlled, architectural garden. Because of the preponderance of reflective materials – steel and water – the position of the sun or of artificial light substantially changes the colour and mood of the garden.

Light and Shade

Making the most of light

Reflecting daylight into dark spaces

Judicious use of light wall colours and ground surfaces, light-coloured, open planting, or lustrous, reflective materials can make the most of what light there is and bounce it in from elsewhere.

Some areas of a garden get hardly any natural light. They include basement areas, gardens surrounded by tall buildings, and gardens heavily shaded by trees. Fortunately, the gloomiest of basement areas can be brightened up without recourse to demolition or artificial light. Even if there is only a 1.2m (4ft) gap between a wall and a basement window, the space can look "green" and have the appearance of being gardened. To assist this, paint the wall white or a light stone colour, or palest grey. Spaces that have very little direct sunlight tend to be quite cool in light quality, so it is better to choose slightly warmer whites and neutrals rather than cool, bluer ones. The effect is also better if the paint is applied to a smooth, rendered surface rather than directly onto rough brickwork.

To soften the stark appearance of the freshly painted wall, introduce plants or trellis, or a combination of the two. Use a light-coloured trellis, perhaps in the form of intermittent pilasters rather than a continuously covered wall. Alternatively, fix tightly strained, vertical, galvanized- or stainless-steel wires as climber supports.

Choose climbers or wall shrubs that can be kept tight to the wall but which have, or can be trained to have, an open habit so that quite a lot of the wall is still visible. Pale-coloured plants, such as golden hop, silver ivy, or evergreen honeysuckle will be cheerful in such an enclosed situation with limited light.

Where there is insufficient room to dig planting holes in the soil, plant in continuous, narrow troughs running the full length of the area, either painted to match the wall or of galvanized steel or other light-reflective material. They will give you maximum soil space without taking up too much valuable ground space. If the ground surface is concrete, cover it with a light-coloured aggregate, such as Cotswold chippings, which is a warm limestone; this again helps reflect warm light into the space.

The planting you choose for a gloomy area must preferably have an open, feathery appearance rather than a large-leaved, heavy one, or have bright pale green foliage. Plants that come into this category and that tolerate shade are bamboos, ferns, the paler-coloured

Using natural light

■ Turn a gloomy basement area into an extension of the garden.

■ Go for light, reflective wall finishes that make the most of what little light there is: use pale-coloured paint on smooth, rendered walls or corrugated galvanized-steel sheeting, for example.

■ Choose light-coloured plants (pale greens, greys, and whites) and avoid heavy, boldly architectural evergreens.

■ Carefully control planting to reveal light-coloured walls or backgrounds.

■ Light-coloured gravel, glassily smooth sheets of water, or pale-coloured paving reflect light from ground level into a space.

◄ **Attracting daylight**
To maximize whatever light is available, position reflective materials on walls and within arches, devise light-coloured (especially grey-foliaged) planting, and use pale-coloured paving or gravel.

► **Restricted areas**
Dark, confined spaces greatly benefit from being surrounded by light-reflective surfaces. Here glass, white-painted walls, and pale-coloured gravel brighten an all-green planting. The light foliage and open habit of bamboo are particularly effective in such a poorly lit site.

▲ Subdued light effects
Old glass backed by silver foil creates particularly mellow, undefined reflections. It recreates something of the charm of distressed, Vauxhall looking-glass so prized in period furniture. Here, a mercury-silvered glass ball on a rod rises out of a box ball surrounded by a sea of *Santolina chamaecyparissus* var. *nana*.

▼ Glass and water
In this corner of a modernist garden, reflective materials predominate in the form of textured, clear-glass paving, still water, and stainless steel. The planting of *Equisetum hyemale* and agave rely on distinctive forms that contrast deliberately sharply with the glossy finishes of the hard landscaping.

▲ Light-reflective screening
This louvred glass screen has separate panels that are movable to catch the light. It makes an appropriately vertical backdrop to the predominately linear and upright planting of *Stipa gigantea*, *Knautia macedonica*, and roses. Light, insubstantial planting of this type benefits particularly from backlighting.

hostas, sweet woodruff, and lovely, bright green selaginella. It is often useful to select taller plants with clear stems up to a certain height, with a foliage canopy at the top. The clear stems stand out against a plain, light-coloured wall without hiding the surface itself. Bamboos can be treated in this way, and their canes in warm gold, black, or green make an attractive pattern against a white wall.

The previous chapter looked at the use of reflective materials when attempting to reduce the visual impact of a boundary (see pp.70–75). Such materials can also be equally useful in reflecting light into a dark space. Mirrors, galvanized steel (particularly corrugated galvanized steel – the roofing material), and water all

have potential to do this. A small mirror pool, in even the most confined space, will reflect the sky, while the glitter and sparkle of even a small fountain or spout will make the most of what little light there is in a particular area.

Corrugated, galvanized-steel sheet used with the ridges running vertically is a particularly useful cladding for a fence or a wall since it catches the light from a variety of directions. It would need to be used en masse to be effective and to look coherent, or it might look like an ad hoc repair. As for most fencing materials, the sheet should be topped with a large capping of timber, 10 x 5cm (4 x 2in), to give it visual substance.

▲ Restricted palette
Grey, white, and green foliage here make a restful and bright combination in an awkwardly shaped, potentially dark passage. The reduction of colour and the retention of large, plain surfaces simplify the design and make maximum use of reflected light.

▶ Lightening a narrow garden
Many town houses have potentially dark areas, often below street level and these are best planted with white rather than coloured flowers. Here white petunias, impatiens, pelargoniums, and lilies are supplemented by white- and cream-variegated foliage.

Contrasting light against dark

In some ways the juxtaposition of light and dark within a garden is more interesting than colour combinations, since it can have year-round effect and is not dependent on the vagiaries of flowers.

Gardens need to make the most of the contrast between light and dark, whether in the use of planting or hard-landscaping, or in the way shadow and light fall on both of these. The greater the three-dimensional interest and the contrast, the more visually successful the garden will be. As in much else with gardening, I am talking here of overall effect rather than small-scale juxtaposition. You should think of the garden as a series of large blocks. Again the analogies of picture-making and stage sets are useful: divide the garden into foreground, middle ground, and distance. There can also be subdivisions within this, although too much fragmentation of light and dark (as with colour) can have too bitty an effect.

Aim to create strong lines or large masses in contrasting, light and dark foliage. Darker evergreens make a useful foil for lighter green or pale grey foliage: for example, the dark blue-green of holly (*Ilex aquifolium* or *I.* x *meserveae* Blue Prince), the black-green of *Quercus ilex* or *Pittosporum tenuifolium* 'Purpureum', or the near-black of low-growing, grass-like *Ophiopogon planiscapus* 'Nigrescens' will create a sharp distinction from pale green plants

such as *Alchemilla mollis* or sedum, or pale grey ones such as *Teucrium fruticans* or *Santolina chamaecyparissus* var. *nana*. Experiment with your own strong contrasts when planning, say, a series of planting groups along the length of a long, narrow garden, dividing it into bays with perhaps the darker plants being used as a taller frame for the lighter ones. This idea works as well in informal and formal layouts.

For formal designs, perhaps the most effective ploy is to frame a secondary garden area through a dark arch cut into a yew or holly hedge. This throws the lighter planting beyond into delicious relief. Again, in a formal or semi-formal context, contrasting edgings to beds can be charming. Think laterally here – the traditional box edging is good, but there are so many other possibilities, either light or dark leaved. *Teucrium chamaedrys* makes a delightful dark green, informal low hedge, as would *Ruscus aculeatus* in a shady site. In the lighter category, silver thyme (*Thymus serpyllum* 'Silver Posie'), lavender, or catmint would make a good edging frame to a darker planted bed or border.

Make the most of contrast

■ Contrasting light against dark in both planting and ornament gives an extra dimension to a garden.

■ Architectural gardens can be more successful when strong colours are suppressed in favour of light and dark shades of a single colour. This shows their sculptural quality.

■ Use dark against light planting to help define the various areas of a garden.

■ Frame the main view of a light garden with a foreground of dark evergreens, or an arched opening cut into a hedge, to throw it into relief.

■ Silhouette bold foliage or an object with a strong outline against a light coloured background of grass or foliage.

◄ **Dark-coloured dividers**
Layers of dark planting contrast well against lighter foliage and flowers. This dark blackish green yew hedge with an opening through it will set off the paler planting beyond and will provide an effective foil for lighter planting in front of it.

▶ **Dark edgings**
A subtle formality has been imposed on these unstructured beds by edging them with the contrasting black foliage of *Ophiopogon planiscapus* 'Nigrescens'. The lines they form are less hard-edged than box. The dark interior of the rustic pavilion that terminates the garden has as its centrepiece a convex mirror whose reflection encompasses the whole garden.

▲ Plant-lined stairway
These steps lead from the dark basement of a
Regency townhouse into a large, light-filled
garden. In this case, the darkness of the entrance
has been intensified by the placing of closely
spaced rows of washtubs planted with bergenias.

▶ Eye-catching foliage planting
It would be hard to imagine a more startling and
contrasting plant combination than *Ophiopogon
planiscapus* 'Nigrescens' and *Stachys byzantina*. For
most purposes, large-scale clumps work better than
spotty mixtures of single plants, because single
plants would tend to merge into an overall grey
when viewed from a distance.

The use of strongly contrasting foliage is especially important in less
sunny northern climes, where bright sunlight itself creates bold
definitions in light and shadow, yet needs to be helped along with
inventive planting. It can also be particularly useful in areas of the
garden where there is very little natural light: for example, in the
approach to a garden from the gloom of basement steps. In such
circumstances, it is better to increase the gloom, so that the contrast
on emerging into the light of the garden itself is all the more
dramatic. Think of flanking the steps with dark pots or containers
filled with large, shady-generating foliage (see above) or arrange

over the steps a trellis or wirework arch planted with climbers, to
create a green tunnel.

A plain, flat wall in shade can be enlivened by creating a recess
lined with reflective material such as mirror, galvanized-steel, or
even shiny vinyl sheeting stretched over a frame. This will be more
effective if the material is faceted to catch any light. There are also
translucent, polycarbonate sheets that can be backlit with exterior,
fluorescent or tungsten light fittings, creating in effect an outside
light box that can be used as a background to silhouette large, dark,
architectural foliage against, as it were, artificial daylight.

◄ Enticing view
Nothing is more inviting than the view through a darkly framed entrance towards a cheerful light garden. Even if the main garden itself is not very sunny, an approach through a darker area – perhaps a green tunnel or a pergola – will, by contrast, make the garden itself seem lighter.

▼ Contrasts of foliage
Light and dark, coarsely textured, smooth, or light and feathery leaves all provide interest in an all-green garden. Here, *Aucuba japonica* 'Variegata' comes into its own as a brightener, while the architectural foliage of gunnera stands out strongly against the smooth texture of yew.

► Optical effects
This faceted mirror niche – intended to represent a cascade – reflects light into a dark corner and is framed by contrasting, dark frostwork in stained timber. Frostwork such as this conjures up visions of caves and grottoes, making the whole ensemble a sort of symbolic representation of the dark and light side of rude nature.

Lighting plants artificially

Creating drama and contrast at night is much simpler than devising such effects during daytime, when sunshine is unpredictable and you have no control of the light source.

Since town and city gardens are more often seen at night than during daytime, it is well worth emphasizing the planting with artificial light. You should, however, avoid bright or strongly coloured lighting – this only annoys neighbours and is usually unnecessary. The easiest form of plants to light are those with bold, architectural foliage set against a plain surface – perhaps a painted wall. Light these from spiked spots in the ground placed so that maximum use is made of cast shadow. You do not need to light a whole garden evenly; in fact, pools of light spaced by areas of dark will be more effective.

By lighting from the ground up, you can cast fantastic shadows and create the somewhat surreal appearance of plants lit from the opposite direction of daylight. To create shadows light plants from the front, and to create silhouettes light them from behind or light a wall or surface behind them so that the plants in front "read" as dark outline. Backlighting tends to emphasize the insubstantiality of plants, whereas front lighting tends to make them look more solid. The best plants to backlight are those with open, elegant profiles: with handsome stems, tree trunks, palms, or grasses, for example. Plants with sculptural forms are modelled and emphasized by front or side lighting.

As a general rule, it is as well to hide the glare of the actual light source. With spiked spots, this can generally be achieved with a

◀ **Angles of light**
Lighting from the ground upwards can highlight plants in unexpected ways, so make use of the wide range of fittings available. These include adjustable or fixed, flush-with-the-ground uplighters, or spiked above-ground spots, to throw light on trees and shrubs, as here, or to mark the line of a path.

▲ **Front and backlighting**
Spiky, architectural foliage here casts wonderfully crazy shadows against a plain wall or fence. A mixture of front and backlighting from ground level makes for dramatic, dark silhouettes contrasted against the brightly lit stems and undersides of leaves.

Lights and lighting

■ When lighting an informal planting, pools of light spaced by darkness are generally more effective than overall lighting.

■ Lighting from the ground upwards transforms a familiar scene and emphasizes the stems and underside of a plant.

■ Consider whether to light planting from in front or behind. Backlighting tends to highlight the insubstantiality of plants and is good for silhouetting grasses or plants with a light, elegant outline. Front lighting is suitable for accenting strong, sculptural forms such as topiary.

■ Exploit shadows projected onto plain surfaces – the farther away the light source, the larger and more dramatic the shadows. The best plants are those with boldly expressed, large leaves or interesting multistems.

■ With the exception of "runway" lighting, it is better to hide a light source behind a baffle, cowl, or clump of plants.

▲ Lighting from within trellis piers
Illuminating trellis piers from the inside shows up the pattern of trellis and also covers a wall with columns of light. There is sufficient spillage of light to accent the surrounding plants subtly, picking up highlights without general flooding.

▶ Nocturnal display
The clear stems of pleached hornbeam are each lit with a single flush from a ground-level, halogen uplighter. This causes the vertical lines of the trunks to be duplicated by shadows, and highlights the plain, cream-painted wall against which the trees are set.

cowl over the lamp itself (many fittings come supplied with these) or a separate, curved, metal "shade" stuck into the soil. The latter can easily be made from cut-out tin painted dark green or black. Alternatively, disguise the light source behind a solid clump of plants, a pot, a masonary pier, or a low wall. You should consider this concealment from several angles. To cut out oblique glare, light fittings may have small, eggcrate baffles under the glass. Some fittings, such as "runway" ground lights, need not be hidden since they are generally used in groups or rows – their visible pinpoints of light being essential to their effect.

With most forms of fitting, the lamp has various angles of beam, and you need to consider how the light will be used before deciding what to choose. Angles generally range from 10 degrees to 50 degrees, and the smaller the degree the narrower and more focused the beam of light. To cast broad shadows from a large plant a wide beam would be best. To throw a thin pencil of light on a wall, or up a tree trunk, a narrow beam is more appropriate.

The distance between the fitting and the plant to be lit is also important. The greater the length, the narrower and more concentrated the beam needs to be. If in doubt, experiment by buying one fitting with several different lamps, with diverse angles and assorted wattages. Usually a variety of lamps are available for the same fitting. The most varied stock is in low-voltage tungsten halogen lamps, and many fittings are available to take them. For these, you need a fitting that has a remote or a built-in transformer.

Recently, LED (Light Emitting Diode) fittings have become available. They have the advantage of a very long life, but generally lamps cannot be changed – a new fitting has to be bought when the lamp actually goes. Their other disadvantage is that the colour temperature of the light is very blue or at best bright white, whereas tungsten light produces a warm colour, which is more flattering to the greens of a garden and matches most indoor lighting. However, the bright whites and blues of LEDs can be very successful for some forms of architectural lighting.

▲ Accenting a tree

This close-up of an uplighter set into decking illustrates a very neat and unobtrusive way to light a tree. The effect of uplighting the under-canopy and trunk of a tree from below can be spectacular, particularly if the canopy is high enough for passers-by to look up into it. For a special occasion, consider switching to coloured gels or coloured lamps. Blue and green are the most stunning.

▶ Subtle lighting effects

Artificial lighting is at its best when not too bright or too obvious. The slots in these masonry piers shed a slightly ethereal wash over the surrounding plants and make the blocks themselves appear to float. The white bark on these birch trees glow magically at night when lit only minimally.

Architectural lighting

A house, garden walls or fences, water, seating, or ornaments in a garden should all be illuminated for dramatic effect not just for visibility.

The floodlighting of a whole house might be too overwhelming in a town or city unless it is part of an important townscape, in which case the lighting would need to be considered as part of a larger scene rather than as an individual building. However, low-key lighting of the private or garden side of a house can be highly effective and ought to form part of the whole garden scene.

Think of ways of making the most of the best features, such as by highlighting the texture of a wall with a grazing light (that is, one close to the surface of the wall). This could emphasize any attractive unevenness in brick or stone or could pinpoint the effect of a trellis grid on a wall, making the laths of the trellis stand out in stronger

relief than during daylight. Alternatively, flank a door or principal window with stripes of light from up- and downlighters in a combined fitting on a wall, fixed maybe 1.8m (6ft) from the ground. From such a fitting, a pencil of light is cast both up and down and several of these can be used like columns or pilasters to draw attention to the whole façade of a building. A similar effect can be achieved by placing uplighters quite close to a building and flush with the ground – again spaced so as to relate to the main doors and windows.

The architectural elements of garden ornament, such as piers, finials, and urns, should be prominently lit so that their key role in a

◄ Lighting from below
Uplighting, the exact reverse of daylight, is perhaps the most exciting way of lighting architectural, sculptural, and geometric forms. Underwater lighting casts a diffused glow.

▲ Striped shadows
A par-38, spiked spotlight placed inside a trellis obelisk casts dramatic shadows against a brick wall. This small terrace is further enhanced by useful ambient light cast through the French windows.

Lighting buildings and structures

■ The lighting of the house and of the garden should be seen as part of the same exercise.

■ Transform the garden façade of a house by marking the main features with pencils of light.

■ Lighting close to a surface – be it a wall, fence, or a trellis – emphasizes its texture.

■ Make use of bold shadows by experimenting with the position of the light source.

■ Consider the various ways of lighting water: for still pools aim for a diffused glow from below or glancing out of the water; for moving water, use underwater lighting to produce animated glitter on the surface.

▲ Repeating pattern
Clever use has been made here of cast wall blocks. The central opening of each block has a nightlight backed by white-reflecting material. Philippe Starck chairs glitter in such moving light.

▶ Warm glow from tungsten and candles
Halogen uplighters highlight the stems of bamboo, while submersible spots provide sparkle to the water spout and a glow to the still water. North African lanterns shed pools of candlelight – the most flattering illumination while dining.

layout is visible at night. Make sure that overhanging mouldings cast deep shadow either by lighting from above (like daylight) or by uplighting. Urns with deeply overhanging rims may need to be uplit from the plinth on which they sit.

To make good use of bold shadows, place a spiked, par-38 spotlight inside a trellis box, for example, and position it so that it casts fantastic, striped, radiating shadows against a plain wall. Geometric topiary against a wall of the house, lit from uplighters in front, can also throw interesting shadows onto the building itself and highlight the effect that the topiary has in complementing the architecture.

Much pleasure can also be derived from well-lit water in a garden. If there is a spout or jet of water, use submersible spots below the source of the spout or jet to create a spectacular sparkle. Alternatively with formal, still pools, lighting from both sides across the width and well below the surface makes for glowing areas of diffused light that ought to be evenly spaced. To achieve a steady, overall glow, try lighting with a continuous strip just below the coping all around the edging of a pool. If the coping projects far enough, a 2cm (¾in) flexible, clear-plastic tube of waterproof pea lights can be concealed. For this method of indirect lighting you must not see the light source, so devise a small, black, metal "pelmet" if necessary.

▶ Submersible spots
Lighting stepping stones across this little pool emphasizes their hovering look and highlights their edges.

▼ Side-lit urns
Two urns, which have been placed between two hedges, are lit from par-38, spiked spots. These are positioned behind green-painted tin cowls, so that the light source is not seen through the hornbeam hedge in the foreground.

◀ A narrow basement area
Designer Ginnie Howard's flat combines classical elegance with modern simplicity. This tiny area has been minimally gardened and brightly uplit by two halogen spots that balance the interior lighting levels.

Lighting a vista

Make the most of a view at night by highlighting its principal points of interest. The fact that the background and surrounding features can remain in darkness makes for exciting possibilities.

At night you can create new emphases and highlight places that are less prominent during daylight. A very confined garden space sited immediately outside a window, for example, can be brightly lit to the same level as the room from which it is viewed. This gives the illusion that the garden is actually part of that room and an extension of the house. Such a lighting effect works particularly well if there are French windows or large sheets of glazing.

Often a large object positioned centrally outside a window or door makes a good termination point. It should be lit dramatically from above or below, using a centrally placed uplighter or downlighter that can be adjusted to the required angle. Side lighting should generally be reserved for less formal situations or for larger-scale lighting schemes.

"Runway" lights set flush with the ground are particularly appropriate lining a path or lawn, to create or emphasize a vista. They should be spaced at intervals of 90cm (3ft) or more – depending on the length of the vista to be lit. If the spacing becomes increasingly close towards the end of the view, an illusion of greater length is achieved. On a path to a front door they provide a guide without being too intrusive. Along a path, use eggcrate or other forms of cowl over the lamps to minimize glare. In such a position, the lowest wattage lamps will be sufficient to provide guiding lights.

Many other different types of lighting are also suitable for lighting a vista, including traditional candles, nightlights, flares, and fireworks. Low-voltage tungsten halogen and mains-voltage

Vistas and views

- Light a vista that is centred on a view from a window, making sure that the light levels outside are similar to those indoors.

- Use front lighting in confined, formal situations. Reserve side lighting for larger or less formal situations.

- Light a path using "runway" lights set flush with the ground. If the path is paved, it is easier to place the lights in a strip of gravel flanking the path. When positioned in grass, the lights should be set flush with the soil so they can be mown over.

- Use flourescent lights, preferably colour-corrected to tungsten, for backlighting or for indirect lighting.

- Vauxhall lights provide a flickering sparkle for special occasions.

◄ **"Runway" lights and border spots**
Guide the way along a path with low- or mains-voltage uplighters set flush. In a bed or border, spiked, above-ground fittings can be used, since they are concealed by foliage.

▶ **A rill of light**
This glass channel in decking implies the presence of water but actually consists only of an etched glass overlay above a cold cathode lighting tube – a form of lighting similar to neon and made up in specified lengths.

◄ **Viewstopper from a kitchen**
This urn on a flint plinth terminates the vista from a basement kitchen/dining-room. It is backed by galvanized sheeting and lit both from above and below. Flanking the urn are fake agaves set on columns and lit from flush uplighters.

► **Vauxhall lights and fireworks**
A path with two flights of steps is here illuminated for temporary effect by nightlights within old Vauxhall lights (the 19th-century equivalent of fairy lights) as well as by fireworks.

tungsten are the main lamp types for most exterior spots. These give a warm colour temperature light in line with most indoor lighting. Alternatively, try flourescent tube lighting, which can be good for subtly diffused panels, for example behind etched glass or opal acrylic. It is particularly suitable for backlighting large lightboxes. Because it is a linear light source, fluorescent tubing or neon is useful for creating directional movement with light – defining an axis or framing a central object. Flourescent tubes can be fitted with coloured filters that warm up or otherwise alter the colour of the light; neon ones are available in a range of colours, but they are

expensive. It is usually necessary to hide a fluorescent tube behind a diffuser or, if used indirectly, behind a pelmet or metal cowl. Make sure you are using fittings designed for exterior use.

For temporary lighting, nothing is more charming than Vauxhall lights – the 19th-century successors to the lamps used in 18th-century pleasure grounds. They rely on tea or night lights (miniature candles in aluminium cases) for their illumination. Their charm lies in the flickering sparkle they give out. Use them on the ground to flank steps and paths (see right) or suspend them on fences, hedges, or trellis to light a vista.

Symmetry and asymmetry
Although the main vista of this Japanese-inspired garden has been lit in a completely symmetrical way, the ad hoc rockwork has been excluded from the balanced effect. A mist machine within the pool makes the submerged lighting especially diffused.

Ground Surfaces

Choosing substitutes for grass and paving

Grass alternatives

Very small town gardens seldom support good lawns, as shade from buildings and trees tends to make the grass thin. Even large, sunny gardens have areas where heavy traffic makes grass impractical.

Nothing beats the rich green of British turf, and in hotter countries there is charm in the coarser texture and varied mix of southern verdure, but even the toughest grass will sometimes not survive. However, you can gain interest and "green up" the garden "floor" using a variety of plant material.

The green category includes box and ivy, which can be kept trimmed in large, flat swathes or can be trained into geometric shapes set in gravel. Although they will not tolerate being walked on, succulents such as sempervivum or stonecrop (*Sedum acre*) can be used as ground cover, too; sempervivum in particular is available in a variety of colours and forms. Both these succulents can, for example, be alternated with gravel or paving (see p.115). Chamomile tolerates light foot pressure and has the advantage of releasing a delicious smell when walked on. In shade, the various ophiopogons, which spread without help, will make broad, solid drifts in time; however, they are not suitable for a busy pathway.

Other plants colonize gravel well, or the cracks between paving, to green up and soften a large area of hard surface. Thymes make a good, spreading mat in these circumstances. It is better to be fairly sparing in its use, though, since a spotty mass of mixed colour in paving can look depressingly messy. Controlled groups of only one or two plants will be more attractive than many mixed varieties dotted at random. Other plants suitable for this type of ground cover are *Erigeron karvinskianus* – a spreading, mound-forming, small daisy that creates a charming foam of pinky white flowers – or, in the right damp circumstances, *Soleirolia soleirolii*, which develops wonderful, low, bright green mounds. Experiment with other plants or leave them to find their own way into the tiniest cracks of soil, in which to form successful colonies.

Many plants grow well in gravel, so it is possible to achieve a seamless flow from gravel to planting and back again. This effect is especially well illustrated at Elsing Hall, Norfolk and at Beth Chatto's garden at Elmstead Market, Essex. Though these are both large gardens, their planting schemes adapt well to a small scale. At Elsing Hall, lush rampant roses trained against the house are mixed with lower plantings that have freely spread. These include eryngiums

◄ **Varied surface without the use of grass**
Contrasting textures of gravel, paving, and swathes of box clipped flat make a shaded town garden interesting without having to resort to a lawn.

▲ **Blurred edges**
In this garden, there is no distinction between paving, path, and planting. One side of the gravel is attractively hidden by an informal grouping of ground and wall planting.

Ground cover and planted hard surfaces

■ Where grass will not grow, "green up" the area with tough plants such as box and ivy, which tolerate dense and dry shade. Sempervivum and stonecrop need dry, sunny conditions.

■ In sunny sites, colonize gravel or paving with plants such as thyme and stonecrop (*Sedum acre*).

■ In shaded, damp sites, *Soleirolia soleirolii* forms a spreading, mounded carpet of bright green.

■ In an all-paved garden, think of dividing up the plot with pockets of low planting that create a grid pattern or define a particular vista.

■ Grass or moss can look charming in the cracks of brick or stone paving, providing it is kept in check.

◄ Defined areas
The various surface divisions of this garden have been clearly demarcated by light-coloured, stone edgings. A slate terrace for dining makes a good hard surface for furniture. At a lower level, there is grass, which is more likely to survive away from the shade of the house.

▼ Medley of surfaces
The delightfully different textures of flint cobbles, stone, brick, and gravel, all colonized by plants, provide a grassless garden with variety and interest.

▲ Box and gravel
A repeat pattern of square, box-edged beds with pyramid bays at their centre set between narrow gravel paths look good on the shaded side of a small town garden.

and euphorbias of various varieties, *Geranium maderense*, *Erigeron karvinskianus*, *Lychnis coronaria* 'Alba', sage, and cistus. The point about this free-flowing method of planting in a small space is that it can be kept vaguely to the perimeter of a gravelled area, but with random incursions into the space. Careful weeding and thinning make sure that plain areas of gravel are retained. Part of the charm of this idea is that the layout changes subtly each year.

When a garden has most of its ground surface dedicated to paving, make sure that there is sufficient interest in colour and texture. A minimalist garden can look good with a single, unadorned surface, but decoration need not be ignored, and many delightful patterns in colour and texture can be achieved in an all-paved garden.

Think of dividing up the area in panels of different materials to create axes that lead the eye in an appropriate direction. A mixture of paving slabs, bricks, and pebbles set in a mortar grid can be highly satisfactory, providing the colour palette is not too contrasting. The passing of time and the accretion of patina, however, will tend to tone down even the most vivid materials. The grid can be used to determine the position of beds or planting pockets within a largely paved area. Such patterns of hard and soft landscaping can be especially attractive when viewed from above.

▲ Weedy pattern
Moss, grass, and weeds have colonized the cracks between this shaded terrace so they emphasize the pattern of the bricks. If kept in check by careful control, these weeds will enhance the effect. Mowing or strimming would be easier than weeding.

◄ Dressing a bed
A planting pocket for a birch tree set in slate paving is topdressed with white pebbles to lighten the effect and make a visual link with the white bark.

▲ Textures in squares
A chequerboard of different coloured gravels, interspersed with plantings of sempervivum and stonecrop (which hardly need water), is divided by black-stained gravel boards. This is a particularly good combination for a dry, sunny site.

▶ Retaining gravel
Stone cobbles in a crenellated pattern such as this make an effective division between gravel and a bed or lawn.

Inventive uses for gravel

Gravel is one of those generic names that covers a vast range of materials of quite different size, texture, and colour. Think of using it in a wide variety of decorative ways within the garden.

Gravel was once one of the staple ingredients of the formal garden. In the 17th century, a parterre of box would not be complete without an infill of differently coloured gravels, which helped to distinguish and enliven the pattern. Today such elaborate pieces of garden embroidery may not often be appropriate, but simplified versions of this idea still work well.

Imagine bold scrolls of box, lavender, or *Teucrium chamaedrys* set within coloured gravel squares – the change of colour being marked by slightly raised bands of brick and by the low hedges themselves. For such a purpose, fine-grade gravel is best. As it will be the colour as much as the texture that creates the effect, use white, black, dull red, or grey gravel or aggregate. Within these basic categories, the odd touches of brighter colour in glass fragments, marble chippings, or painted gravel can be sparingly introduced. To achieve a very fine line between colours, use metal lawn edging, which is available in flexible, off-the-peg lengths.

The design of a parterre can be very simple and might be effective if disproportionately large for the space available, to give the appearance that it is a section of a much larger design. This would also help to give grandeur to a tiny plot, rather like the bold cropping of images in Japanese wood-block prints.

Another 17th century idea – the Parterre à L'Anglais – consisted of a flat design carried out in only mown grass and gravel. Again, this can very effectively adapted to a modern garden using either a formal, symmetrical design or a boldly cropped, asymmetrical one. Lay metal edging between grass and gravel for really sharp definition. In this case, pale neutral gravel looks particularly well with grass. Even with a more complex design, a single colour of gravel would be more successful. Such ground patterns could well be enlivened by the odd vertical plant: for example, by *Cupressus sempervirens* Stricta Group or *Juniperus scopulorum* 'Skyrocket', or by cones of box or yew.

Gravel can make a statement in a garden even when incorporated very simply. For example, a broad, serpentine path through swathes of colour-controlled planting would give a bold pattern to a garden. For the best result, choose a colour that

◄ Simple variation on a traditional parterre
The elaborate baroque curves of a 17th-century Parterre de Broderie are here simplified to four scrolls of box set in squares of differently coloured gravel, bounded by brick.

▲ Carpet edging
A pattern not unlike the border of a carpet marks the join between grass and a planting of catmint. The composition is enhanced by light-coloured gravel laid between a line of bricks and slabs cut on the diagonal.

Designing with gravel

■ Use coloured, fine-grade gravel to demarcate the various sections of a parterre or knot of box, lavender, or *Teucrium chamaedrys*.

■ Light-coloured gravel will define the pattern of a Parterre à L'Anglais – a flat design in cut grass and gravel.

■ Gravel creates large, plain surfaces instantly – use it for a path that needs to make a bold statement in a garden or to create geometric areas as a contrast to informal planting.

■ To create texture on a flat surface, rake the gravel in an interesting pattern.

■ The "floor" of a garden can be composed largely of gravel studded with other materials that help define it: for example, set paving of various types flush with the surface.

contrasts strongly with the general colour of the planting. Alternatively, a sharply defined rectangle of gravel would give counterpoint to an informal, wild planting as well as providing the contrast between geometry and disordered nature that is required to make most gardens a success.

Consider ways of making the most of the varied textures of gravel and larger pebbles. The Japanese way of raking gravel into beautiful patterns around rockwork, for example, can be adapted to suit other styles. This might mean raking bold stripes to emphasize the width of a garden or to reinforce a directional movement

towards a viewstopper. It might comprise only an arrangement of differently sized pebbles set in raked gravel. The great thing about this idea is that it is easy to rearrange.

Gravel can be used as the basic substrate of a garden design, studded as it were with other materials: paving slabs, wood blocks, stones, and plants in either formal or informal compositions. In these circumstances you might think of introducing varying scales of similarly coloured material, perhaps larger sizes in the foreground with smaller-scale pea gravel farther away, to create an illusory perspective as well as a satisfying variation of texture.

◄ Bold statement
A serpentine path of light-coloured gravel and limestone chippings (referred to as Cotswold chippings) makes a dynamic route through a garden of well-coordinated foliage.

▼ Rearrangeable pattern
Raked gravel, Japanese style, around a carefully chosen rock adds texture and linear interest to a minimalist garden.

► Variations in scale
Large pebbles set in mortar form the risers for shallow gravel steps and provide an interesting pattern in the path.

An informal mixture
Thymes and achillea form an
attractive composition in gravel
interspersed with pebbles and
timber planks. The seamless
movement from one material
to another makes for a varied
progression through the garden.

Patterns in hard surfaces

Texture, colour, and pattern are as important when designing paving as when arranging a planting scheme. Varying the material or laying it in an unexpected way adds interest and diversity.

Think of the ground surfaces in a garden as you would the floor of a room: the best schemes have interest without being too busy. As with a patterned carpet, areas of dense, complex pattern ought to be contrasted against larger swathes of plain surface. Make sure that the dominant colour or texture leads the eye in the right direction. A path, for example, need not be strongly defined along its length, but could be banded across its width with a contrasting, more prominent material. This provides pace and movement. Random divisions, such as the series of diagonally cut slabs interset with ammonites (see right), give a cheery quirkiness quite different from the cool, elegant effect of straight lines.

If you are introducing several materials to a design, make sure that they work together yet contrast against the colour of planting. Paving should usually be quite clearly differentiated. Often the same material in different textures can be effective, such as the contrast of cut against riven Yorkstone. The way that a stone or cast-concrete slab is pointed will also have a considerable effect on a pattern: for example, flush joints homogenize the surface, while sunken joints or those with broad pointing define the separate slabs. Very inexpensive, cast-concrete slabs can be made much more interesting by banding them with a brick set on edge between each joint, to create a crisscross grid. Alternatively, try giving a larger expanse of

Pattern on pattern
This variety of materials including pebble inlay, gravel, and paving slabs makes for a rich effect. A thin covering of water brightens the colour in the pebble inlay, rather as if it were varnished.

Paving possibilities

■ The ground surface of a garden is like the floor of a room. Contrast plain surfaces with patterned ones to avoid an indigestible effect.

■ Intersperse inexpensive, cast-concrete slabs with more interesting materials such as brick.

■ Emulate the pebble inlays of southern European countries to achieve a richly decorated ground surface.

■ Unexpected combinations of old and new materials are well worth exploiting.

■ Make the most of the natural patina that comes with age – even on modern, reconstituted paving materials.

Shape, colour, and texture
Alternating wedge-shaped stone slabs and inlaid ammonites makes a jaunty pattern in a slightly twisting path. The combination of shapes and textures helps give a sense of movement to the path.

plain paving a frame made up of a brick course, in which the bricks have their longest side set vertically, rather than horizontally.

Ransacking history and looking at different national and regional paving types provides inspiration, too. The pebble inlays of Spain and Italy can be readily adapted. They generally use contrasting colours – often small, black-and-white, river- or sea-washed stones set in diamond or star patterns, or in baroque swirls. Sometimes these are laid within a broad grid of dressed stone and diversified with black-slate inserts. In Britain artists such as Maggy Howarth specialize in wonderfully complex designs of pebble inlay, employing a wide range of subtle colours – a sort of updated Roman mosaic, but using natural stones rather than glass tesserae.

The wide variety of regional paving types are all part of a vernacular tradition that can be incorporated into modern schemes. They include: slate laid on edge rather than flat; slate in herringbone pattern; pebbles set in mortar to create gulleys flanking paths; and the use of small, square cobbles. Sometimes unexpected combinations of old and new work well, such as the mixture of ceramic mosaic with granite setts and gravel (see right). Inlays of stainless-steel lines look good set flush with the surface of cut stone. Coloured, engraved grooves forming abstract patterns add a subtle pattern without being distracting within the overall garden scene (see p.127).

A large part of the charm of many natural materials is the way they weather – mosses, lichens, and moulds helping to diversify their surfaces and enliven their colouring. Even cheap cast-paving slabs mellow with age. They do this more speedily and satisfactorily if they have an open-textured, porous surface rather than a glassy, smooth one. Pressure washing is death to a patina, so avoid it if you want to build up a richly aged surface.

▲ **Fluid lines**
The grain of these long, narrow paving slabs, as well as the way they are cut and set at an angle to the direction of the path, makes its serpentine passage especially dynamic.

▶ **Pleasing bird's-eye view**
A complicated scheme of blue mosaic and cobbles laid in gravel form a delightful composition that scarcely needs planting. Consequently, it looks good year-round, but especially in winter when herbaceous foliage has died back.

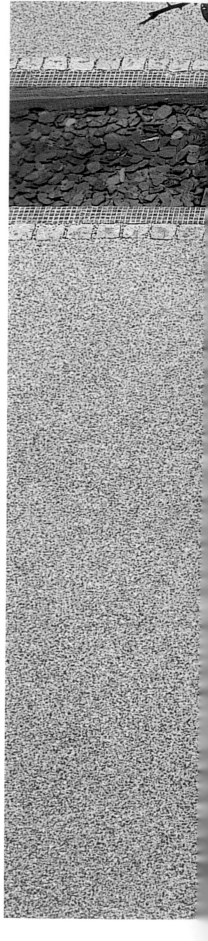

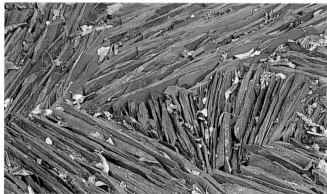

◄ Single-colour pattern
Slate laid on edge in an informal, herringbone pattern is a modern variation on a design previously used in the house for the backs of fires or hearths.

▲ Complex inlay
Sliced log sections and ceramic ones set among plants in fine gravel create a highly complex pattern that needs to be offset by a plain surface such as grass.

◄ Concrete and brick
Concrete slabs can be transformed by banding them with brick inserts. This means the joints "read" as a strong grid pattern.

▲ Framed pattern
The smooth stone border provides both a frame to the herringbone pattern, and, in practical terms, supports the small, shaley stones.

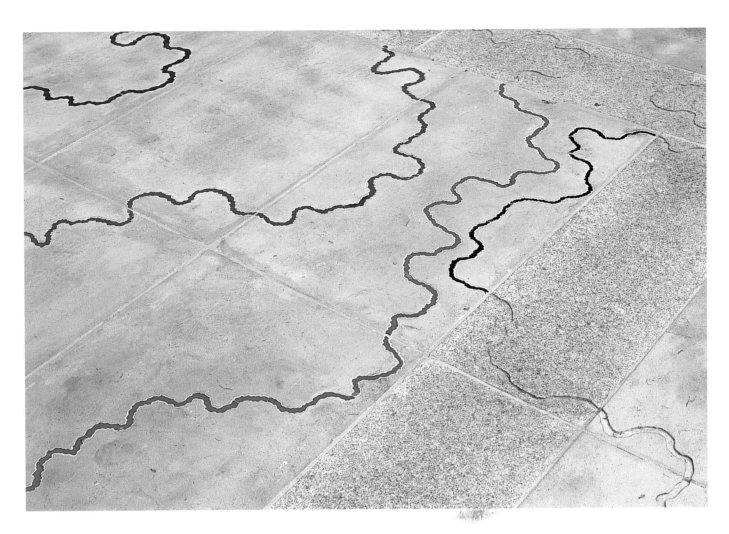

▲ Engraved, linear pattern
Very closely jointed, cut-stone paving has been laid here so that the blocks themselves are virtually seamless. They therefore provide a good foil for the main pattern of incised, coloured lines.

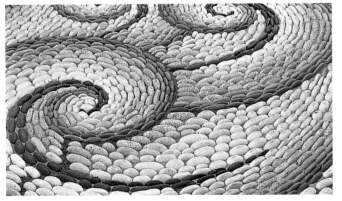

► Pebbles as mosaic
Having been carefully graded for colour and size, pebbles have been placed to form a pictorial design by the mistress of pebble-work, Maggy Howarth.

► Concentric circles
A radiating pattern of pebbles laid in mortar would make a good junction between two paths or as the centrepiece of a circular garden.

**Precise edges with
rough surfaces**
Riven Yorkstone stepping-stones
across a formal canal create a
textural contrast with the glassy
smooth surface of the water. The
edges have been machine cut so
that the blocks themselves have a
geometric precision essential for
a formal effect.

Planting for overhead effect

A garden may be viewed not only from ground level but also from above, perhaps from an upper window. If there are high walls its planting, meanwhile, may be looked up at as well as down onto.

The plan of a garden really has a major impact when you are looking down onto it from above – may be from an upstairs room or from a raised terrace or balcony. This is where strong structural planting and clearly defined divisions really come into their own. A bold pattern of box edging or well-trained topiary will look good from above, as its form can easily be perceived. Strong forms read without help but complex, informal planting requires clear space around it to display the design most effectively. Use grass, gravel, or paving to create plain areas that act as a frame for luxuriant disorder. Even where soil is not available, such as half way up a house or garden wall, planting can still be introduced either using carefully trained climbers or by placing it on shelves or bracketed troughs.

A series of paths, viewed from above, can look like a painting by Piet Mondrian, and you can derive a similar pleasure from their abstract composition. This is easy to do on paper at the planning stage. In fact, adapt a section of an actual Mondrian painting if inspiration fails. Space between the linear grids forms a patchwork of grass or beds. This idea works particularly well with vegetable gardens, which for convenience need a network of narrow paths. The rows of planting and the pole supports used in a kitchen garden make for a particularly attractive, bird's-eye view.

A common problem in towns is that the only garden space is at basement level while the principal rooms are on an upper floor. Where an external staircase links the two areas, you can colonize the staircase itself with plants in pots. Utilize the access to adjacent walls

◄ Two and three dimensions
Gardens with strong architectural form look well from above. In this case a combination of flat-pattern and three-dimensional architecture make for a particularly varied scene.

▲ Planting surfaces
A staircase to a basement area has been integrated into the garden by providing a platform for pot plants. It also gives access to lead-covered, hanging shelves, which hold a changing display of pot plants. Towards the bottom of the staircase, a large landing creates seating and further staging for larger containers.

Looking down and upwards

■ A bold pattern of box or clearly defined topiary will look good when viewed from above, especially if it is positioned against wild or luxuriant, informal planting.

■ Kitchen gardens with their clearly marked path and bed structure look particularly well from above. Poles and supports project the ground plan into three dimensions

■ Devise grid-like patterns for ground plans and take inspiration from geometric abstract art.

■ Make use of architectural features such as external staircases to provide access and support for high wall planting.

■ Project planting upwards so that it is more visible from above. This can be achieved by suspended planters or by creating supports such as pergolas or tunnels for climbers.

▲ Geometry contrasted with luxuriant planting
The best place to "read" a pattern in box edging is from above. Here, the hedge pattern makes a good foil for the informal planting of roses and peonies.

▶ Bird's-eye view
The contrast between plain and complex areas shows up well in this overhead picture. The different "rooms" and levels each have a distinct character and are marked by changes of ground surface and furnishing.

provided by the staircase to make shelves for plants in individual pots that can be changed and rearranged through the passing seasons. Plants with trailing habits can be useful here: try ivy-leaved pelargoniums such as Blanche Roche (white flowers) or 'Vectis Blaze' (darkest purple), or – the staple of hanging baskets – trailing ivies and the charming, grey-leaved *Helichrysum petiolare*.

Even quite serious gardening can be achieved in suspended troughs, supported from a wall or walls on stout, metal brackets. Imagine surrounding a small service area with a sort of suspended box knot garden, so that a planting of box hedges and topiary in elongated, continuous window boxes would surround four sides of a light well and be fixed at the level of, or just below, the main reception-room windows. You effectively lose the dark area below, even though the light well is reduced only by the depth of the planters, perhaps 25–30cm (10–12in).

Furnish the walls surrounding a sunk area with strong-growing, preferably evergreen climbers planted at ground level. They can be supported on vertically or horizontally strained wires or on trellis. In a sheltered, warm position, plant attractive *Trachelospermum jasminoides*, with its white, scented, jasmine-like flowers in summer. The hardier *Holboellia coriacea* is another vigorous, evergreen climber good for camouflaging drainpipes and other eyesores.

A further way of providing overhead planting is to build a simple tunnel pergola, perhaps constructed of lightweight, metal arches or more substantial timber. These look good, both from above and from inside the tunnel. To avoid creating dense shade, they can be quite lightly planted and the supports quite widely spaced. Suitable quick-growing climbers are *Wisteria sinensis*, *Vitis labrusca*, *Lonicera japonica* 'Halliana', or for a more formal solid effect train hornbeam to create a clipped, green tunnel.

A linear plan
The pattern of paths and plants in rows make a delightful overhead composition on the lines of abstract geometric painting. Projecting the design upwards with canes and plant supports makes the whole effect three dimensional.

Water as a reflective surface

No space is too small to accommodate at least a little water. Both still and running water can be used to reflect light and glitter into a dark garden or to create mirror images of nearby objects.

◄ Mirror pools
Very simple pools of still, reflecting water lined with black material make wonderful outdoor mirrors. The key to their success is good water quality achieved by ultraviolet filtration or chemical treatment, or both. The circulation of water needs to be discreet so as not to disturb the surface too much.

► Plants in ponds
Plants improve water quality but they need to be kept in check so they do not take over and reduce the reflective area. This pool shows the effect of a sunken water level and stepping-stones cantilevered over their supports, making the slabs appear to hover over the water.

Water is a medium with an infinite range of colour possibilities. It is affected by both the colour behind it and the colour of what is reflected into it. To achieve the best still-water reflections in a pool, line it with black-painted render, butyl liner, in-situ black resin coating, or black tiles. The choice will to some extent depend on the scale and the shape of the pool. A large or irregular pool would be effective in butyl or with in-situ black resin. Smaller, geometric ones would work with tiles or painted render.

To retain the blackness in a pool liner, you need good-water quality and a consistent cleaning regime – by regularly removing leaves and deposits from the base, for example. On a small scale, it is easy to treat water by filtering it mechanically and pumping it through a ultraviolet filter to kill algae and so on. Provided there are to be no plants in the water, you can also use chemical treatment similar to that for swimming pools.

Mirror pools need strict attention to their edges and to the level of the water in relation to the pool perimeter. A full-to-the-brim appearance can be striking, particularly where grass is planted right up to the water (see p.138, top). The turf should be retained from the water using a black metal upstand. When cutting the grass, you have to be careful to avoid too many clippings going into the water. Any that do should be fished out.

The sparkle of water

■ To enjoy the best still-water reflections, fit a black liner in a pool.

■ A mirror pool can have its water level set close to the surface, and this creates a frameless effect.

■ A water level that is lower that of the surrounding ground gives a more three-dimensional, framed appearance.

■ An informal, irregularly shaped pool is seldom successful in a small space; it needs a larger setting.

■ Avoid over-planting a small pool; keep plants in check and leave plenty of open water.

◀ **High water level**
The junction of grass and water almost at the same level makes for a surprising but delightful, artificial effect seldom found in nature. A black, metal or plastic upstand forms the edging between the grass and water.

◀ **Chameleon-like qualities**
Water is a versatile medium that adapts itself to a variety of settings. When more or less divorced from planting, a raised tank filled almost to the brim with water can be transformed into a piece of architecture – the watery surface being more connected to stone and glass than to the natural world.

▶ **Formal pool surrounded by informal planting**
This pool not only lightens the effect of mostly green planting but also supplies a formal geometry that helps offset irregular plant compositions.

Perhaps less visually exciting but more practical are stone or brick copings around mirror pools. These again can have the water surface as close to the top as possible.

There are circumstances where a dropped water level works well: with boldly overhanging copings, for example, or where stepping-stones sit on smaller bases so they appear to float over the water (see p.137). A slightly lowered water level gives a more three-dimensional effect and emphasizes and distinguishes a pool from its surroundings. To achieve a really glassy effect you need no turbulence, so any circulation of water needs to be discreetly done at a low level or through buffles.

Informal, irregularly shaped pools are much more difficult to make visually satisfactory and I personally think they should not be attempted in a small garden, where definite geometric shapes are more appropriate. Irregular, "natural"-looking pools really work well only on a large scale where they can appear part of a landscape or wider garden scene. Water features such as horse, mill, or farm ponds are usually man-made, and their shape is determined by convenience rather than by design.

The main point of pools in small and especially in dark gardens is to reflect light into them: when you are close to the water and at the right angle, you should be able to view the overhead sky; at a distance, you should see reflected objects. Make sure there is a beautiful sculpture, urn, or small building close to the pool edge or actually rising out of the water to take advantage of this.

Aquatic plants can also make for beautiful reflections and help keep water clean, but they should not be planted too densely. You should ensure large areas of water are clear of planting to make the most of water's beautiful, reflective quality.

For really spectacular reflections, exploit the lighting of plants and objects at night. Underwater lighting destroys reflection, but is good for highlighting the sparkle of moving water or for a diffused glow in still water.

Water as a reflective surface 139

Complementary planting
If a large pool is planted with discretion, the planting on its banks can then be quite complex. As the pool here includes few plants, there is ample room for reflections of both the sky and the planting around the edges.

Theatrical Effects

Adapting ideas from stage designs

Rearranging a garden for a party

Whether in town or the country, a garden comes into its own for entertaining. Exploit lighting within this extra space, rearrange furniture, provide shelter, and add temporary decoration.

One of the chief functions of a garden in the 17th and 18th centuries was to provide a setting for social events of all kinds. Grand fetes, theatrical performances, firework displays, musical entertainments, and dinners were all given in garden settings which were sometimes quite radically modified for the day. It is still possible, with comparatively little effort, to give a garden a festive air, and it is much more easily transformed than an indoor room.

For a large drinks party you need space, as well as most probably lighting, and you might require heat or shelter. In very small gardens, it is possible to roof over the entire space with a canvas awning fixed to the top of the walls (if they are high enough) with ties through screw-eyes permanently in place. You might need a central support like a tent pole, fitted into grass or into a tube liner such as are used for rotary washing lines (see opposite). You might also consider hiring or buying one of the many types of gas or electrical garden heater now available. It will, however, be the decorative changes you make that will have the most impact.

Vauxhall lights (see pp.105 and 149) have the most magical effect. Use them to delineate architecture by placing them on windowsills or on battens arranged round doors; by hanging them in the spaces between trellis; or by lining walks and steps. Ideally they need to be used in quantity, but as they are available new as well as old that need not be a problem. The nightlights that illuminate them last for a long evening. Put electric, spiked spotlights into soil to light areas of the garden that are not normally visible. The main rule is to hide the light source itself, either in foliage or behind pots or tin cowls.

Garlands and festoons have always been associated with festivities, and they make especially good garden decorations. Sling them between trees on a large scale with a wide span and deep curve. The traditional way to make them is to tie evergreen leaves in small bunches around thick rope: good shrubs for cutting are bay, cherry laurel, and Portugal laurel. The festoons should be fatter at the base of the curve, narrowing towards the top. Flowers or fruit can be added for colour, if required. Florists' wire or thin, green

◄ Dressed for a party
The simplest garden layouts make the best party setting. Here a raised terrace at the end of a garden provides a good outdoor dining-room. It is divided off from the rest of the space with clear-stemmed limes, hung with large festoons, which could be of cut foliage or long stems of ivy.

▲ The garden as a marquee
The awning covering the whole of this very small garden space is fitted to screw-eyes in the top of the side walls and is tied through eyelets in the polypropylene canvas. The pole supports the centre of the awning.

Transformation scenes

■ In a very small garden, dispense with a marquee by roofing over the entire space with an awning.

■ Temporary lighting by candlelight and electricity is the cheapest and easiest way to transform a garden at night.

■ Large garlands and festoons are the outdoor equivalent of flower arrangements indoors. They give a festive air and to help define areas of the garden when slung between trees.

■ Create temporary enclosures for a party using trellis panels backed by foliage.

■ Devise different areas in a garden for outdoor dining so that your guests can move about to experience the whole garden. Work out the best positions for sun, shade, night, and day.

horticultural wire is best for tying the decorations. Hang festoons on fences or around doors with vertical pendants of the same material framing the sides. A hint of Grinling Gibbons can be added by using thin strips of lead, 2.5cm (1in) thick, bent into fluttering ribbons and attached at the suspension points. Wrapped in low-voltage pea lights, such festoons also look good at night.

Rearrange furniture both for use and for effect. Windsor-type chairs painted dark green were the most common sort of movable garden furniture in the 18th century, and they still look good ranged in formal groups or dotted randomly about a garden. Non-matched sets can be bought cheaply and painted a discreet blue-green. In modern settings, nothing looks so good as the elegant, Philippe Starck, clear-plastic stacking-chair, which blends beautifully into a

garden setting. Even in quantity these "invisible" chairs don't make a garden look cluttered.

To arrange a terrace for entertaining, you need to conjure up a sense of enclosure and protection, even if it is only notional. You also require a flat, preferably hard surface, especially if your guests are to dine there. Create an enclosed space if one doesn't already exist by wiring together 1.8m (6ft) square panels of trellis stained in receding colours, such as dark green, grey, or faded blue, to make a good background for foliage. For temporary effects, cloth them in cut hops or wired-on cut foliage from oak or any other small-leaved tree. I think it is pleasant to design several such "rooms" within a garden for guests, to give them a choice of views and vistas to explore.

▲ **The garden as theatre**
A semicircular hedge of hornbeam, cut with arches framing urns, is backed by an outer hedge of x *Cupressocyparis leylandii*. Box balls represent footlights, though the urns are side-lit from between the two hedges. Copies of 18th-century Windsor chairs are ranged to complete a circle for guests.

▼ Eating area
A garden with a clear level deck
and a sense of enclosure is ideal
to transform into an outside
dining-room. Make sure that
any pots and other types of
container are moved back to
achieve sufficient chair space.

▲ Temporary adjustments

The movable elements of this south-facing, 2.5m (8ft) wide terrace can be easily rearranged to provide more space for tables and chairs. Topiary in pots is particularly useful in helping define a garden "room".

▶ Partition for a party

Artificial festoons of bay leaves give a festive appearance to grey-stained trellis behind which a holly hedge is being trained. Trellis can be put up as a temporary screen and gives the illusion of enclosure.

▶ Nocturnal display

Vauxhall lights lit by flickering nightlights are hung in the spaces between trellis backed by yew, to enliven it at night. The glass pots, which constitute Vauxhall lights, are hung on home-made wire hangers.

A *coup d'oeil* or viewstopper

Every garden needs one or more objects that terminate the view and attract the eye. Such a *coup d'oeil* could be a piece of sculpture, an urn, a found object, or a piece of spectacular topiary.

An object does not have to be grand or expensive to act as the focal point of the garden, but it does need to be striking and carefully placed in its setting. It could be quite a simple cutout such as a piece of fretted plywood in the profile of an urn, obelisk, or figure. When seen from even a few metres away, such a conceit can work, by deceiving the eye into thinking it is the real thing. A cutout is especially effective if it is backlit using the painter's technique of *contre-jour*, so that it appears as a silhouette. Such an effect can be achieved without natural or artificial backlighting if a dark-painted cutout is placed against light-coloured planting or a pale-painted wall. To have the maximum impact, choose an object that has a bold, easily identified profile – the more baroque the better.

Alternatively, think of adding to a flat cutout in *trompe l'oeil* painting (see opposite). This effective way of achieving a three-dimensional illusion always looks better in grisaille (monochromatic grey) than in multicolours, so select neutral stone colours and make the overall shading light, with minimally defined shadows. The cutout can be quite sketchily painted and in fact works better that way.

A novel way to achieve a similar result is digitally to enlarge a scan of an engraving or a photograph and mount it on waterproof plastic; then add further weatherproofing with matt laminate. The scans can be done on a cutout or as a large rectangular backdrop. Digital printouts can also be made onto self-adhesive vinyl and stuck directly onto a smooth wall or a piece of waterproof board – a technology used for advertising hoardings that is relatively cheap. You could produce large blown-up photographs, but I personally think the more abstract effect of enlarged engravings is more amusing, making reference as it does to the 1950s Italian designer Piero Fornasetti.

Amusement should, perhaps, be one of the prime motives when devising a viewstopper. Think of inventive ways of conjuring up an object without the real thing: the painted plywood cow on p.152 is a good example. You could make a sculpture that is partly flat and partly three dimensional, such as the basket of foliage also on p.152. This has been devised not only to catch the light and create strong shadow but also to have a comic-book simplicity that will

◄ Terminal feature

The end of a garden is here defined by a trellis screen framing a cutout basket of foliage in plywood. This viewstopper creates interest and distracts from what is beyond. A sense of buildup is also formed by a series of oval-edged lawns.

▲ Convincing illusion

A flat cutout, painted figure makes an inexpensive substitute for "real" statuary, especially if you make it yourself. This is a modern version of the ancient practice of *trompe l'oeil* in gardens, which was begun by the Romans and has remained popular ever since.

Eye-catchers

■ Every garden needs a focal point or viewstopper, but it does not have to be an expensive object. Experiment with simple shapes cutout of plywood.

■ Digital technology makes it possible to produce large blow-ups that can be used as backdrops to a garden scene.

■ When choosing a background for a sculpture, pot, or urn, make sure that it is positioned against a plain surface and framed in some way.

■ Modern castings generally look much better with the patina of age. There are various ways to induce this artificially.

■ Where a garden contains more than one focal object, make sure each is screened from the others.

◄ Rural touch

A series of flat plywood cutouts have here been skilfully assembled to create a three-dimensional grazing cow. Even though it is very simplified, when seen at a distance this illusion really works, partly because the form of a real cow would be broken up by its black and white markings, reducing it to shapes that are difficult to decipher.

▼ Effects of light

The play of strong light on any form simplifies and reduces it to broad masses and makes detail invisible. Bold, almost crude, cutouts are often more striking than the real thing, especially when seen from some way away.

▲ Improvement with age
Informal planting benefits from a focal point, in this
case provided by sculpture. A modern, cast-stone
figure of 18th-century style is greatly enhanced by the
patina of age. Here lichens have colonized the surface
reducing the harsh effect that new material often has.

"read" well at a distance, in a way that a more highly detailed and
less boldly cut subject would not.

Many off-the-peg casts are available based on original works of
art, ranging from classical to modern. The disadvantage of newly
cast stone is that it doesn't look very good initially, but it can
eventually develop a fantastic patina. In most damp and shaded
positions, the aging process takes no more than a very few years
and can be speeded up by the application of yoghurt, liquid
manure, or patent patinating preparations. If you have the money, a
bronze casting with a beautiful, green patina, or the pale surface of
oxidized lead, cannot be bettered.

Whether in a formal or informal setting, choose a plain background
consisting of planting or architecture, or a combination of the two.
Decide whether the backdrop needs to contrast with the object or
complement it. Most objects benefit from a frame of some sort, and
this could comprise a niche, or a notional version of one, or it could
be a foreground frame that concentrates the eye: flanking planting,
a path, a gateway, or a pergola, for example.

Avoid being able to see too many objects in one glance. In fact
there is a charm in discovering viewstoppers gradually as you
progress. A caught glimpse that only hints at an object is a good
way of introducing a sense of expectation and surprise to a garden.

Correctly scaled sculpture
Pergolas must be terminated by a view or an object that is appropriately proportioned within its framed setting. This figure has sufficient presence, but not too much bulk, to be an ideal viewstopper to a substantial pergola. Here a plain background is essential since the pergola and its planting are visually complex.

Scenery "flats"

Frame a garden scene with a series of timber "flats", which are the sidescreens of a piece of stage scenery, or use stage properties to cheer up a dreary corner in your garden.

Although the use of painted canvas "flats" has already been discussed under "Receding screens" (pp.46–51), it is considered differently here in that its incorporation into a garden is inspired more directly from the theatre and is even more to do with illusionism. In the 17th century, the theatre had a clear influence on attitudes to gardening: for example, the great plantsman of the period, John Evelyn, claimed that London gardens were "all marchpane and pasteboard smelling more of paint than of plants and gardens." ("Marchpane" is an archaic word for "marzipan", and Evelyn was making reference to the elaborate, architectural food decoration of the period.)

Every garden includes places where nothing grows well, where the outlook is unprepossessing, and where a little, lively theatricality would not go amiss. In some areas, such as narrow, dark basements, this sort of peepshow approach to gardening is the best and easiest. In such a setting, try to emphasize the gloom and make something of it; for example by introducing a pseudo-grotto with a series of fretted pieces of ply painted in graded-stone shades or dark greens, to create depth and mystery. A mirror reflecting a blank wall could form the background (see opposite); avoid directing the mirror at a window. Use simple, toothed or stalactite cutouts to create a cave and frame them with fretted, dark, leafy "foliage". The layers can

Basement areas where plants will not flourish.
This is quite literally pieces of stage scenery made of painted waterproof ply. The whole *trompe d'oeil* appears to be in three dimensions because the "flats" have been spaced one slightly behind the other. The illusory effect can be greatly enhanced by lighting either from below at the front or between the various layers of the scenery.

Staged for effect

■ A theatrical approach to garden design is particularly appropriate in places where even the most stalwart plants find conditions uncongenial.

■ Adapt ideas of illusionism from the stage to create an entirely artificial garden decorated with flanking scenery "flats" and a painted or cutout backdrop.

■ Juxtapose the real and the artificial, and frame the junction with real planting round the edges of a *trompe l'oeil* scene.

■ Suggest three-dimensional figures, carving, or moulding by simple fretwork and sketchy painting.

■ Use theatre-style footlights to illuminate a scene masked by shell-shaped shades

Illusion of depth
This symbolic representation of a grotto in fretted and painted ply has its far layer backed by a mirror. Because only a small arch of mirror is visible, very little of the real scene beyond is revealed, yet the number of intervening layers is doubled so the "tunnel" seems much deeper.

▲ **Trompe d'oeil mixed with reality**
A combination of the fake and the real, the classical and the prosaic, makes a good joke. Here a real wall, shelf, and onion strings are turned into a surreal scene by the addition of flat-painted busts and urns.

► **Cohesive setting**
Dividing a wall into defined bays with trellis helps give structure to a garden and, against a white wall, provides illusory depth to the boundary. The freestanding, foreground arch adds a proscenium-like frame to the vista.

be quite close together. You could also take advantage of any under-street cellar doors to extend the vista through into a real "cave".

One of the best conceits is to juxtapose the real and the fake. Think of making a cutout frame for a particularly good specimen plant or an attractive urn or sculpture. A trick much used in the past was to conceal some edges of *trompe l'oeil* within a three-dimensional, architectural arch and hide the base and other edges with real foliage.

The representation of three-dimensional objects by clever use of flat cutouts makes it possible to devise quite elaborate architectural effects without high cost: for example, carving and elaborate mouldings can be suggested by quite sketchy execution. The Gothic gateways on p.160 are a good example of this. At a distance, they look like elaborately carved arches with pineapple finials, and even when viewed close-up the knowledge that they are false is not disconcerting. The finials are made up of four flat profiles, two of them notched together at right angles, while the other two are cut

into four and glued at 45 degrees into spaces between; the same idea can be used for a whole host of shapes, regular or irregular. Although such an object requires ingenuity to design, many three-dimensional shapes can be suggested following this technique. All you need is a fretsaw or an electric jigsaw, together with waterproof ply and glue of an outdoor type.

The way the "flats" are lit, both by day and night, is an important consideration. Where you have a series of solid "flats", place ground-level spots between them, using different wattage lamps to achieve layers of graded light; set brighter lights in the distance and lower-wattage ones in the foreground. Otherwise, position footlight-style spots in the front of the scene. The spots themselves can be hidden behind traditional, shell-shaped shades, which are still available in brass or other metals. They look good in the garden painted dark green. If there is no direct sun and therefore no shadows, ensure that there is sufficient colour contrast between the various layers during daylight to make them stand out.

▲ Stage arch

Gothic arches and Chinese Chippendale trellis create an *Alice in Wonderland* sense of unreality in this all-white rose garden. The very simplified construction of the fretted arches gives an appropriately theatrical look to the scene.

▶ Change of role

The simplest of scenic devices – a series of diminishing panels – is here carried out to great effect with the most basic materials. A completely plain, white background transforms a tree fern into a leading character, as it were, singling it out from the rest of the planting.

False perspective

Ground plans can be devised using converging beds, or lines of trees; parterres can be squeezed or narrowed in the distance; and colour can be used to simulate aerial perspective.

◀ **Disguised rectangle**
Make the most of a long, narrow garden by dividing it up with a series of projecting spurs of hedging or trellis, or a combination of the two, to create a sense of recession. Zigzag lines in planting or paths are a successful way of focusing the attention and creating a sense of movement.

▶ **Perspective trellis**
This type of trellis is easy to make yourself. Losing the edges of the trellis behind a frame of ivy increases the illusion of depth.

French town gardens in the 18th century were renowned for their spectacularly elaborate latticework that dissolved the walls of adjacent houses with false perspective of a very architectural kind: arch succeeding arch and illusionistic columns apparently disappearing into the distance. Today, simpler ideas are generally favoured.

A sense of recession can be achieved with the architectural elements of a garden, such as the use of converging lines for trellis panels. Two sets of vertical laths screwed to a wall or fence, and fixed increasingly close together, are an effective method of framing a central object and making it look farther away. Trellis pilasters made up of closely spaced, vertical laths can be ranged across a wall; the pilasters are increasingly narrow and positioned closer together towards the centre. They can also be in reducing heights.

Repeating a series of verticals on a pergola will engender a sense of depth when viewed along its length. Even rows of posts enhance perspective in a garden, and these can look particularly good running down the centre of a bed to provide a repeating structure. They need only a lead capping as decoration or a simple ball finial, and should be not less than 12.5cm (5in) square. Their height should be determined by their setting, but rising out an herbaceous bed they may need to be 1.5–1.8m (5–6ft). Double rows or more, spaced at 1.2m (4ft) intervals, make a delightful space frame that

Illusory tricks

■ In various really simple ways, straight lines of trellis laths can be made to create false perspective.

■ Gradually reduce the width of pilasters, and position them closer, as they disappear down the garden. The same idea of diminution into the distance can be applied to beds, lawns, and paths.

■ Simple, repeating verticals such as posts or substantial plant supports within a bed or lawn exaggerate the depth.

■ Adjust the layout or spacing of planting to achieve the illusion of greater distance.

■ Imitate the effect of aerial perspective by colour-grading planting from dark or warm colours in a foreground to cool, pale ones farther away.

gives perspective to a lawn. Provide the posts with simple, decorative finials and paint them off-white or pale grey, so that they show clearly against grass, gravel, or underplanting.

A tapering lawn, bed, or path will have a similar effect of false perspective and is much more difficult to detect as a deception, unless you have a bird's-eye view. More sophisticated variants on this idea can also be tried. A series of decreasing-width, lozenge shapes in hedging such as box, for example, has the added attraction of a zigzag dynamism, drawing the eye to the apex of the vista. The spacing in lines of trees, standard roses, or other significant, structural repeat planting can be reduced as they recede.

▲ **A sense of recession**
The repeat pattern of a series of posts, as in this substantial pergola, helps give depth to a garden. The contrast in colour of the pergola against the distant arch – light and bright in foreground, dull in distance – also puts illusory space between the two objects.

▲ **Tree-lined path**
The same repeat pattern, in this case provided by the stems of stilt hornbeams, makes a short, grass walk appear to recede. A distorting mirror at the end of the path punches a notional hole through the boundary wall, extending the vista still farther.

The same ideas can be used in layouts of informal planting. Bigger clumps of large, well-spaced plants in the foreground of a scene can be contrasted against smaller and lower groups set closer together in the distance – perhaps with the beds themselves narrowing. This works not only with straight lines but also with irregularly shaped or serpentine beds.

This effect can be further enhanced by the way colour is used. In a long bed that is primarily viewed from one end, think of introducing dark, rich or bright, light tones in the foreground; these should gradually give way to paler planting with less vibrant colour in the middle ground of the bed, and move to cooler, greyer planting in the distance, to simulate the appearance of aerial perspective – the increased haziness due to particles in the atmosphere making the distance of a landscape look increasingly bluer or greyer.

Have fun devising planting schemes to achieve such aerial perspective. Grey-foliage plants with those producing small, white or blue flowers are good "distance" plants: try catmint, lavender, santolina, *Tanacetum densum*, or *Festuca glauca*, for example. Larger-leaved, dark-coloured plants, which are suitable in the foreground, include *Macleaya microcarpa*, *Cotinus coggygria*, *Heuchera sanguinea*, and *Atriplex hortensis* var. *rubra*.

Neo rustic
A convex mirror, its edges concealed by a twigwork-and-cork frame, reflects the whole of a small, Regency period garden and brings glitter to the inside of a rustic summerhouse. Such a combination of textured, rustic materials and smooth mirror would have appealed to the early 19th-century taste for its startling contrast.

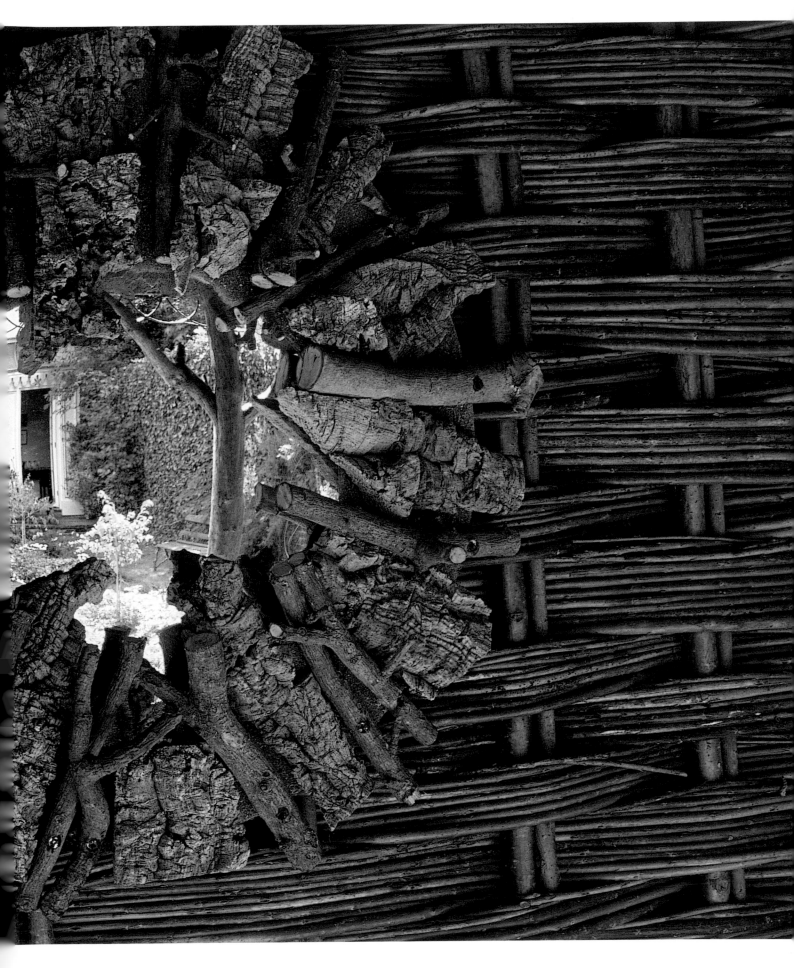

Juxtaposing differently scaled objects

Playing around with expected proportions in a house or garden creates surprising effects. Large objects or plants in tiny spaces can assume a grandeur quite unrelated to the real extent of the place.

The scale of the various parts of the garden and of the house is related to the size of humans. Doors and gates have a certain anticipated height and width; seats are, within a small range, the same distance from the ground, and so on. Everything has an expected scale, so it can therefore be fun to make subtle – or not so subtle – adjustments to the size of things. Although such changes apply particularly to the hardware of gardens, the same tricks can be pulled off in the way plants are chosen and juxtaposed.

Something as simple as altering the width of decking or the size of gravel can have a considerable impact: for example, narrow decking set in a small space has an enlarging effect. This can be intensified if very overscaled pots (as on p.171) or other large, simple objects, such as piers or large, solid blocks of planting, are introduced. Although they take up a lot of room, they break up the space, making it more intricate, and consequently it is harder to appreciate the real size.

The contrast of objects much bigger than expected with those much smaller is a conceit that can often be put to good use. An underscaled door or opening in a wall or hedge can be installed for effect-only as a fake – it will look much farther away than it really is. For this illusion to work, other objects with an expected scale, such as a table or chairs, have to be distanced from it. However, you might want to mix scales up for fun, as on p.169, where a very low, wide door is placed close to a seat of the correct height.

Even minute town gardens can benefit from one hugely oversized object. Put an enormous urn on a massive pier into a space 5m (15ft) square to achieve the illusion of grandeur. Not much else would be needed. On the same principle, one large chunk of topiary or a single, large, spreading tree, suitably pruned to let in light, makes a small area feel bigger, because this dominant object becomes the main focus of the scene. The umbrella-trained catalpas, which are ubiquitous to tiny Provencal courtyards designed

Bigger or smaller than expected?

■ Deceive the eye by adjusting the size of a feature that has an expected human scale, such as a door, gate, or seat.

■ Disregard "appropriate" scale; rules are made to be broken.

■ Contrast overscaled objects with ones that are underscaled, setting them in close juxtaposition.

■ Introduce one hugely overscaled object, tree, or shrub into a small town garden to gain an effect of grandeur.

■ Use large, boldly textured foliage in the foreground of a scene to contrast with smaller, smoother-textured foliage in the distance.

◀ **Distorting proportions**
Overscaling in the foreground and underscaling in the distance are basic ways to increase the apparent size of a garden and to add amusement. In this garden, a door that is smaller than expected is approached by a narrowing path, which is flanked by box balls in reducing diameters.

▶ **Unexpected proportion**
A low, wide door in a garden pavilion gives a surprising scale to the building itself, and when contrasted against a seat of normal height makes for a dilemma as to which is the correct scale. The eye can detect quite subtle distortions.

for summer shade, are an example of how successful can be this disregard for "appropriate" scale. Often such situations occur by chance: a small shrub grows into a massive tree, but its presence transforms a garden from the pedestrian into the special. Often it is these quirky accidents that give a garden character, and they should be worked round and incorporated rather than removed.

In a small space, it is generally better to use smooth, untextured surfaces and very small pea gravel, which would be more enlarging than a coarser grade. However, if large gravel in the foreground is separated by some intervening surface with smaller gravel in the distance, the smaller gravel will look surprisingly further away.

This same idea can be applied to formal and informal planting: diminishing sizes of topiary balls, cones, or other shapes flanking a path, for example, or the gradation of leaf texture from coarse to smooth in informal planting. Though this sounds far-fetched, it is an idea that has long been current. Descriptions in the 17th century of formal, architectural gardening make reference to the careful use of texture in topiary being meticulously carried out in different plants for "green architecture" reasons: holly and laurel for coarse surfaces; box, yew, and phillyrea for smoother ones. A good, 19th-century recreation of this style survived at Brockenhurst Park in Hampshire into the 20th century.

Consider also the way bigger features are used, and how delightful it is to move from a low, dark tunnel of greenery, trained over a light iron frame or timber posts, into an open, sunnier area.

▲ Contrasting components
A low, dark tunnel of foliage forms a good approach to a garden or a section of one, as it causes the open, airier part to appear bigger and lighter. The introduction of a gateway leading to a further division in the garden adds an extra dimension.

▶ Think big in a small space
By contrasting narrow decking with very large containers in a confined space, this small roof terrace seems very spacious. This "trick" works for two reasons: firstly, the block-like containers divide up the space into more complex, smaller areas that confuse the eye; and, secondly, the floor appears bigger because of the disparity in scale between its planks and the pots.

Tiny garden with numerous distortions

The foreground gravel in this miniature plot is of a bigger grade than the background. The planting reduces in scale and substance; and the trellis-encased yew blocks are set closer together at the rear. The eye takes all this in without, perhaps, recognizing the exact nature of the trickery.

Index

Page numbers in *italics* refer to picture captions. Those in **bold** refer to main entries

Acknowledgments

All photographs are by Marianne Majerus, with additional design and location credits as follows.

Front cover: Gardens & Beyond
Back cover: Marie Clarke at Clarke Associates

2 Declan Buckley; 5 Chloe Wood; 6 Del Buono, Gazerwitz Landscape Architecture; 7 Kathy Miller; 8–9 Susanne Blair; 13 George Carter; 14 above Miranda Holland Cooper, below George Carter; 16 Declan Buckley; 17 Barbara Hunt; 19 Diana Yakeley; 20 above Michèle Osborne, below Christopher Bradley-Hole, RHS Chelsea 2004; 21 Christopher Masson; 22–3 Tom Stuart-Smith, Laurent-Perrier Harpers & Queen Garden, RHS Chelsea 2001; 25 Julia Brett; 26 Gardens & Beyond; 27 George Carter, Raf Fulcher, Elizabeth Tate, sculpture by Elizabeth Tate, Allegorical Garden, RHS Chelsea 1997; 28 Joe Swift; 29 above Julie Toll, below Gardens & Beyond; 31 Anthony Collett; 32 above Michèle Osborne, below Joe Swift; 33 Gardens & Beyond; 34 above Christopher Masson; 35 Bunny Guinness; 36 Barbara Hunt; 37 George Carter; 39, 40, 41 Christopher Masson; 42–3 Bunny Guinness; 44–5 George Carter; 47 Sally Brampton; 48 George Carter; 49 George Carter, Raf Fulcher, Elizabeth Tate, A Vision of Versailles, RHS Chelsea; 50–1, 53 below George Carter; 54 above Declan Buckley, below Chloe Wood; 55 George Carter; 56 above and below Susanne Blair; 57 Ali Ward, paintings by Mark Maxwell; 59 Claire Mee Designs; 60 Gardens & Beyond; 61 Ruth Collier; 62 Michèle Osborne; 63 George Carter; 66–7 Peter Chan & Brenda Sacoor, Silverstream, Weybridge; 68–9 Claire Mee Designs; 71 Christopher Masson; 72 above and below as back jacket; 73 Sarah Hosking; 74–5 George Carter, Christie Sculpture Garden, RHS Chelsea 1999; 76–7 Declan Buckley; 79 Marie Clarke; 80 above George Carter, Raf Fulcher, Elizabeth Tate, below Philip Nash, Steel and Glass, RHS Chelsea 2004; 80 Christopher Bradley-Hole, RHS Chelsea 2004; 82 Dominique Lubar; 85, 87, 88 George Carter; 89 below Heather Wilson; 91 Hotel Tresanton, St Mawes, Cornwall; 92 Stephen Woodhams; 93 George Carter; 94 Michèle Osborne; 95 Phil Jaffa with Patrick Collins, Knightsbridge Urban Renaissance Garden, RHS Chelsea 2004; 97 George Carter; 98, 99 Claire Mee Designs; 100, 101 above George Carter; 103 Claire Mee Designs; 104, 105 George Carter; 106–7 www.spidergarden.com, Japanese Garden, RHS Chelsea 2000; 108–9 Christopher Bradley-Hole; 111 Del Buono, Gazerwitz Landscape Architecture; 112 above George Carter, below Gardens & Beyond; 113 Christopher Masson; 114 below Gardens & Beyond; 115 above RHS Chelsea Flower Show 1998; 118 Chloe Wood; 119 above Lucy Sommers, below Peter Chan; 120–1 Julie Toll; 123 Bunny Guinness; 124 Terence Conran & Nicola Lesbirel, Laurent Perrier Harpers & Queen Garden, RHS Chelsea 2004; 125 Michèle Osborne; 126 above Marney Hall, RHS Hampton Court 2002, centre Paul Cooper, below left Claire Mee Designs, below right Christopher Masson; 127 above Phil Jaffa with Patrick Collins, Knightsbridge Urban Renaissance Garden, RHS Chelsea 2004, centre Jane Hudson & Erik de Maeijer, pebble mosaic path by Maggy Howarth, Cancer Research UK Life Garden, RHS Chelsea 2004; below Marc Schoellen; 128–9 Del Buono Gazerwitz Landscape Architecture; 132 Tom Stuart-Smith; 133 Paul Thompson; 134-5 Mark and Anne Reeder; 137 Declan Buckley; 138 above Christopher Bradley-Hole, "Garden From the Desert", RHS Chelsea 2003, below Jacques Wirtz, Banque Générale du Luxembourg; 139 Kathy Miller; 140–1 Dan Pearson, Merrill Lynch Garden, RHS Chelsea 2004; 142–3 Del Buono, Gazerwitz Landscape Architecture; 145, 146–7 George Carter; 148 Christiane Schwartz-Majerus; 149 above and centre George Carter; 152 above George Carter, Raf Fulcher, Elizabeth Tate, A Vision of Versailles, RHS Chelsea, below George Carter; 153 Jill Billington; 154–5 Paul Thompson; 157 George Carter; 158 cut-out heads by Louise Dowding, Yews Farm, Somerset; 159, 160 George Carter; 161 Paul Cooper; 162 Mary Payne; 164 Chloe Wood; 165 Bunny Guinness; 166–7 George Carter; 169, 170 Bunny Guinness; 171 Diana Yakeley; 172–3 Woodpeckers, Warwickshire.